MW00715112

Ana
23 March '18

READYMADE BUSINESS OPPORTUNITIES

READYMADE BUSINESS OPPORTUNITIES

A Guide to Options within Self-Employment

Greg Clarke

KOGAN PAGE

First published in 1994

Apart from any fair dealing for the purposes of research or private study, or criticism or review, as permitted under the Copyright, Designs and Patents Act, 1988, this publication may only be reproduced, stored or transmitted, in any form or by any means, with the prior permission in writing of the publishers, or in the case of reprographic reproduction in accordance with the terms of licences issued by the Copyright Licensing Agency. Enquiries concerning reproduction outside those terms should be sent to the publishers at the undermentioned address:

Kogan Page Limited
120 Pentonville Road
London N1 9JN

© Greg Clarke 1994

British Library Cataloguing in Publication Data

A CIP record for this book is available from the British Library.

ISBN 0-7494-1264-X

Typeset by Saxon Graphics Ltd, Derby
Printed and bound in Great Britain by Clays Ltd, St Ives plc

To Charley

Please note that United Kingdom telephone numbers are due to change on 16 April 1995. After that date, please check any numbers in this book that you plan to use.

While every care has been taken to ensure the accuracy of the contents of this work, no responsibility for loss occasioned to any person acting or refraining from action as a result of any statement in it can be accepted.

Contents

1

Introduction

You may be considering self-employment, but perhaps you do not have enough specialised knowledge of a sufficiently distinctive product or service which you could provide to customers.

Obviously, before you can even start to think seriously of self-employment, you need a good business idea; one where you can provide, at a profit, a product or service to the public and/or to other businesses.

Self-employment, being your own boss, can be attractive, but you probably also realise that it can be risky. Many businesses fail, particularly in their early years. No form of self-employment is without risk. But perhaps the odds can be moved in favour of success if your business is based upon providing a proven product or service, marketed under a reputable 'parent' company's name or trade mark.

This approach to running your own business should certainly save you the time, bother and expense of having to introduce and establish your own brand new name in the market. It should also save enormously on research and development costs, as well as the trials and (perhaps disastrous) errors which appear to be inherent in the start-up and running of new business ventures by fledgeling business owners. Having a parent company intimately dependent in some way on you achieving success may help to provide you with support, advice and encouragement in what might otherwise become an isolated existence.

There are a surprisingly large number of such 'readymade' business opportunities through which you could enter self-employment. They will all rely, in one way or another, upon your ability to sell the products or services of another company, trading under a name other than your own.

At the core, though, you remain a self-employed business person. As such, your own commercial success, or failure, also hangs upon your own business and management capabilities, self-motivation and dedication.

So, your own business – under someone else's name – could become a viable proposition. Certainly it should be worth exploring further. It is hoped that this overview of the options available will enable you to form your own more considered opinions.

Whether you are considering running an agency, a distributor-ship or a dealership, joining a multi-level marketing or direct selling scheme, thinking of taking up a franchise, entering the financial services industry, buying an existing business, consider-ing a public house tenancy, even a management buy-out or management buy-in, or freelancing from home under contract, reading this book should be your first step.

Readymade Business Opportunities is designed to be a concise and easy-to-read volume of basic facts and tips, providing a useful introduction to understanding each of these types of business arrangement. However, each chapter also contains signposts to sources of further information and advice which you are recom-mended to seek and consider before determining a final course of action.

The contents are designed for any fledgeling entrepreneur wanting to move straight into a known market with an established business name, or into a new market with someone else's unique product or formula for success, who needs to know where to begin.

2

Ingredients for Success

Whether you can build a successful business, even from a readymade business opportunity, is going to depend on the quality of all the assembled and developed component elements, combined in the right proportions as ingredients for the venture as a whole.

These ingredients for success may be summarised as follows and we will then examine each one in more detail:

- You
- Support
- Market awareness/market intelligence
- Viable product/service
- Route to the market
- Trading name
- Good parent company
- Financial and organisational controls
- Funding
- Business planning
- SWOT analysis

You

- Your own personal temperament, attributes and abilities;
- Your capacity to learn and adapt;
- Your ability to plan, implement and control the business in terms of your resources *vis-à-vis* time and money;
- Your own personal objectives and clarity of purpose;

- Your ability to capitalise on your strengths and minimise the effect of your weaknesses;
- Your attention to the administration and recording of financial information and your skill in managing finances;
- Your willingness to work hard;
- Your desire to succeed.

Be aware that personal characteristics and capacities are often the deciding factor in determining the success of a business venture. It requires a fairly obsessive temperament and a capacity for dealing with stress.

Many people in business claim that their prime motivation is not money. In fact, many might earn more elsewhere, especially considering the effort and risks involved. They are concerned more with the nature of the activity and the sense of involvement and personal satisfaction.

Being self-employed is a way of life, not just a job. Understanding yourself, your motivations, strengths and limitations will be a crucial ingredient for both initial and sustained success. Working successfully alongside an established company and its management will require a positive approach to the relationship by both parties. Because of the particularly controlled 'partnership' nature of the relationship in franchising, that subject is covered further in Chapter 4. However, many of the comments there also apply equally well in any self-employed situation.

Everyone has different personal strengths and limitations. Ask someone who knows you well to assess your personal characteristics objectively, using the following score sheet. Request that they use a cross to score you 9 for an obvious strength and 1 as the lowest score along the line. Then score each aspect for yourself, as objectively as possible, by putting a circle around a relevant dot on each line.

Where your circles do not match the crosses, check with the other person about their reasons for scoring you as they have. Also, reconsider your own estimates in the light of the other person's opinion.

Use the results of this simple checklist to examine your motives for self-employment thoroughly. Plan ways in which you can build on your strengths and, importantly, how you will minimise the effects of your own limitations upon your business.

Personal characteristics score sheet

[Score 9 for any characteristic of obvious strength; 1 as the lowest score. Mark only one position along each line.]

Characteristic	1	2	3	4	5	6	7	8	9
Ability to work hard	.	.	.	.	.	.	.	.	.
Desire to succeed	.	.	.	.	.	.	.	.	.
Management ability	.	.	.	.	.	.	.	.	.
Financial awareness	.	.	.	.	.	.	.	.	.
'People' skills	.	.	.	.	.	.	.	.	.
Determination	.	.	.	.	.	.	.	.	.
Energy level	.	.	.	.	.	.	.	.	.
Ability to cope with stress	.	.	.	.	.	.	.	.	.
Independence	.	.	.	.	.	.	.	.	.
Ability to listen to others	.	.	.	.	.	.	.	.	.
Level of self-esteem	.	.	.	.	.	.	.	.	.
Ability to analyse risks	.	.	.	.	.	.	.	.	.
Ability to manage own time	.	.	.	.	.	.	.	.	.
Creativity/Initiative	.	.	.	.	.	.	.	.	.

Support

- On the one hand, you will need to be self-sufficient and resourceful enough to keep driving the business, but you must also be able to rely on the support of those around you – essentially, your family.

- You should also be willing to seek out and use any external agencies able to offer knowledgeable support and/or advice.
- The parent company should be willing and able to assist you in a number of ways and this could be a real strength.

Market awareness/market intelligence

A good business idea and a good trade name are two of the obvious essential ingredients for business success, but the fact remains that without customers you do not have a business at all. The market should be clearly identifiable and quantified.

You should know what sort of customers you are looking for, where they are and how to find them.

You need to know how their needs are currently being satisfied, or whether there is a genuine gap in the market which you can exploit. If there appears to be an opportunity, research further; is there in fact a market in the gap?

As a fledgeling business person, be wary of revolutionary new or unproven products and concepts. Ask for, and heed, objective advice from as many sources as possible. Talk to your local Training and Enterprise Council (TEC); make contact with the Chamber of Commerce. Seek out other trustworthy business owners in the same, similar and competing markets and find out as much as you can about their experiences.

Even general polite enquiries to other operators, relevant trade associations and the editors of trade journals can be enlightening, particularly during the early stages of your research. Of course, you will have to decide at each stage of your research how much of your own plans you are going to divulge to each person.

- You will need to be aware of exactly what the market is that you will be in. Is your market (and profit) to be found in just selling products or will you in fact be providing a service, the quality of which enables you to charge a premium? For example, if you intend running a pub, your customers will almost certainly consider that you are providing a hospitality/ leisure service and not just selling a range of drinks and snacks.

- Thorough analysis of the market must be undertaken. Meaningful research should identify the current size and potential for growth of the market as a whole and your part in it in particular.

  Research should also show up the observable trends and those which may reasonably be predicted when all factors which can possibly influence the market are taken into account. Such factors may include social, political, economic and technological change, the activity of competitors, and the uses to which the product or service may be applied; ie the opportunities and threats facing the business must be clearly identified and dealt with.

- This also means that the market 'width' *and* 'depth' should be identified, defining the types and numbers of prospective customers, where they can be found, and how their needs for the product or service are currently satisfied; ie who and what provides the competition for the amount of customers' money that you want to be spent on your products or service?

  Again, what market will you be in? A luxury fountain pen may have less to do with ball-points and fibre-tips than with cigarette lighters, silk scarves and cuff-links in the adult gift market. In this case, packaging, presentation and perceived value become more important than price alone. It is also an example of where the value of a respected brand name scores heavily.

- At what stage is the overall market in terms of its life-cycle, ie is it expanding, relatively stable or declining?

Viable product/service

- The product or service must offer a unique selling proposition, ie a valid reason for customers to buy from you rather than from other companies competing for their business in the same market.
- The margin you can obtain must allow for your viable business survival, development and growth. An old adage says that profit is made when you buy and realised when you sell. Even providing a service on a commission-only basis requires close scrutiny of your true costs, expenses and commitment of time, in order to assess the final value to you of each sale.

- The product or service ought to be clearly safe and ethical, with no harmful effects on the environment.

Route to the market

- Knowledge of how competitors make their sales.
- Will you be doing the same? Can you afford to be different, to have a different approach? It may be a different approach to the market which provides your unique selling proposition.
- Territorial considerations may well need to be taken into account. Where do other similar businesses in the parent company's network impinge upon your scope for activity? Where might you impinge upon theirs? What are the marketing benefits of being in the network?

Trading name

- Is the trading name already well known and established?
- Does the trading name have a good reputation?
- If relatively new, is the name relatively easy to remember? Is it catchy and easily identifiable with the type of business being promoted?
- Will the name last the life of the business and allow for strategic market development if necessary?
- Is there a logo which helps to identify the brand of product or service? A logo is a visual device or design which is particular to its owner. It can help to differentiate the product or service in the market-place.

It is important that the right to use the trading name and/or logo is clearly established; that is, that the parent company has clear title to use the name and/or logo and the right to assign it for your use. It is a good idea to check the Trade Marks Registry at Companies House to make sure that the logo or name has been registered by the company. Many businesses do not have a registered trade mark, so you could have less protection than you may be led to believe.

Also, as you will not be trading under your own surname as your business name, the law requires that: your name and that of any other owner(s) of the business must be stated on all business letters, written orders for goods and services, invoices and receipts, and on written demands for payment of business debts. An address must be given for each person named, at which any document relating to the business will be accepted, and you must display your name and address prominently at your business premises or at any place to which your customers will have access.

Once you are trading, if anyone with whom you are discussing business asks you to disclose your own name and address, you must do so immediately in writing. If you are setting up as a limited company, you are required to register with the Companies Registration Office. When you submit your choice for your own business name, along with the other documents required for registration, the name will be accepted unless: a) there is already another company with that name on the Register; b) the Registration Office considers the name offensive, obscene or illegal.

The Department of Trade and Industry (DTI) controls the Companies Registration Office and also publishes its 'List of Sensitive and Prohibited Names'. This contains certain words and expressions which will require specific consent from the DTI before they may be incorporated into the name of the limited company.

You may consider starting as a limited company by buying one already with a name 'off the peg', ie a readymade company, one which already exists but is no longer trading. These are sold by company registration agents, and if you wish to change the name you and your fellow directors simply pass a special resolution to that effect. This must then be sent as a typed document to the Companies Registration Office, together with the required fee. Assuming that the name you have chosen is acceptable, you should receive a Certificate of Incorporation on Change of Name.

For many fledgeling entrepreneurs wishing to trade as a limited company, this can be the cheapest and quickest form of doing so. The names of local company registration agents can be found in Yellow Pages, or you can seek advice from your accountant.

For details on the rules on company names, two free books explaining them are available from Companies House: *Disclosure of Business Ownership* and *Control of Business Names*.

Companies House also operate a telephone-only service whereby you can find out whether the name you are considering for your own company is already in use by someone else.

Good parent company

- Undertake your own thorough research into the company: its background, true size and financial standing, its reputation in the market and its reputation among other 'licensees' in its network.
- Who are its principal officers? What are their backgrounds and experience? Have they been involved in previous business failures, or ever been made personally bankrupt?
- Who are the true owners of the business, ie the major shareholders?
- What initial and on-going backing or support can you expect, and how will this be achieved?
- What initial and on-going training can you expect, and who pays for the costs involved?
- What communications will you receive on financial information, market intelligence, performance data?
- What administrative systems will you be expected to operate? These should be as straightforward as possible and directly relevant to your own needs. Accurate and timely administration of the business will be essential, but beware of becoming an unpaid administrator or analyst for the company's sole benefit.
- Will you receive help to draw up your business plan? You should be responsible for constructing your own business plan, but realistic sales forecasts and some market research data should be forthcoming from the company, using proven results gained elsewhere and clearly showing any assumptions which have been made.

Financial and organisational controls

- Having well-thought out management information and financial control systems;
- Adhering to those systems;
- Taking time out to review progress regularly, understanding what the figures mean and responding effectively to them;

- Having a detailed and comprehensive business plan constructed before you start and reviewed regularly;
- Monitoring performance against the business plan, responding to variances to secure the progress of the plan, or indeed amending the plan in order to achieve your business and personal objectives;
- Being proactive and driving the business forwards, rather than reactive after unforeseen events, ie accelerating along the straight, but slowing down and changing gear before the bends! It is your responsibility to control the pace and direction of the business.

Funding

- Skilful planning and control of cash flow is absolutely essential.
- Knowledge and use of the most suitable types of funding available.
- Forward planning of all financial requirements to ensure that your selected types of funding are used most cost effectively, ie the right amounts from the right sources, at the right time and at the right price.

   Note that in any new business start-up the margin for error is slim. You are strongly advised to consult an accountant who is experienced in the field you wish to enter.
- You will need to identify clearly and cost out the resources required for adequate distribution and selling, advertising and promotion. How much of these costs will you be expected to finance yourself and how much will be covered by the company under whose name you are trading? When would the customers be expected to pay for delivery, installation etc?
- If premises are required, you will need to identify the best location, cost, size and facilities required. In retailing, it is often said that the three most important secrets of success are: location, location and location!
- Optimum pricing strategy should be clearly thought out to maximise viable returns, compatible with your medium- and long-term business development plans as well as the need for profit, and cash, in the short term.

- The high street banks may not necessarily be your best first choice for help in financing your business, as explained in Chapter 3. However, even if you think that you need no further financial assistance, you will most likely require the facilities of a business bank account. It is therefore wise to meet the commercial small business managers of each of the main banks. It is often sensible to hold your business account completely separate from your personal finances, and you should in any event draw up a business plan. The banks each offer free information packs to enquirers. These are designed to assist in the task of clarifying your strategy and devising a coherent plan, before you commit any money or time to the proposed business. You could then ask your chosen bank if it would consider supporting, say, half the funding you need in your first year. At the prospect of its own financial involvement, the bank should be rigorous in its consideration of your plans. Remember, the bank manager will first of all assess you – your character and competence, as well as your capital.

  Find an experienced accountant to help you deal with your financial affairs. He or she should also be able to offer advice on alternative sources of funding, grants and business start-up loans, as well as on your overall plan and its costings.

Funding and sources of finance are covered in more detail in Chapter 3.

Business planning

Your business is more likely to be successful if it is planned thoroughly at the outset and if the plan is monitored regularly as you go along.

The business plan is for your benefit. It should take you considerable time and effort to piece it together. However, better to screw up and throw away a few pieces of paper containing plans that you realise will not work, than to waste several years of your life, money and domestic harmony living through ill-considered pipe-dreams.

The business plan is comprised essentially of six Ms: mission, management, markets, margins, money and methods.

- **Mission** means making succinct statements of the objectives of the business, statements of what you want your business to be known for. Defining your mission statement forces you to identify the purpose of the business clearly. It can also be used to give an unambiguous signal of your policy and direction to others involved in your business, your financiers, employees, customers, suppliers, family and friends. It is the yardstick by which you can measure the success of the business. As the old story goes: when you are up to your waist in muddy water trying to fight off alligators, it is difficult to remember that your objective was to drain the swamp!

  A good mission statement should be SMART – Specific, Measurable, Achievable, Realistic and Time-bound.

- **Management** means you – your CV giving details of your age, education, experience, skills and abilities. Your profile should also list details of your personal means, your property, assets, liabilities and guarantees etc. Similar information should be recorded for any partners or fellow directors of the business. Essentially, you are analysing your own strengths and weaknesses; showing how you can capitalise and build on the strengths, and how the effect of weaknesses can be minimised by the strengths of others.

- **Markets** means proving the need for your business. This section covers all the combined research and resulting forecasts for sales. It should identify direct and indirect competitors, analysing their strengths and weaknesses. It should state your unique selling proposition, the competitive edge by which you intend gaining market share.

  The marketing mix is often summarised by the use of four Ps: Product, Price, Place and Promotion. You should be able to describe the benefits of the product clearly, state the pricing policy, the method of distribution and selling, and determine the optimum advertising/promotional activity required.

- **Margins** means how your business will make profits. It should cover costings and forecasts of income, monthly for the first year and quarterly for the second and third years, ie forecast trading and profit and loss statements.

  The effects of payments out from the business against the

inflow of money coming from sales or investment into the business must be planned for and realised ahead of time, ie a forecast cash flow analysis is essential. Profit may mean different amounts to different people – you, the Inland Revenue, investors etc – and might only be calculated after some period of time. Cash is what pays the bills as they fall due. Many a profitable business has collapsed for the want of immediate cash.

These financial forecasts should include an analysis of the break-even point, ie the point at which sales are sufficient to cover all the costs. Break-even can be calculated by the simple formula:

$$\text{Break-even} = \frac{\text{Overheads}}{\text{Gross profit margin \%}} \times 100$$

This also shows that the break-even point is dependent not only on the difference between your selling prices and direct costs (those costs which vary directly with output) but also on total overheads (all the fixed costs which are payable irrespective of output).

Therefore, any change in any of these figures forces a change in the break-even point. Thus it is wise to calculate the break-even point arising from a number of 'what-if' scenarios involving variations in gross margin and your projected overheads. Balance sheet projections will also be required.

- **Money** means funding requirements for set-up, survival, development and growth. The funding proposals should take account of your own capital investment and that of any other private investors. The financial forecasts detailed under 'Margins' should clearly identify the nature and amounts of funding required at different stages of your start-up, ie capital investment, long-term loan and/or short-term overdraft facility. You should be able to identify clearly the specific purpose of any external funding and the length of time for which it is required. You will have to determine realistic repayment proposals to which you agree to be bound and state what security you or the business can offer as collateral.

You should also seriously consider what types and amounts of insurance cover you will need. It is worthwhile taking advice from several brokers, your accountant and other business advisers.

- **Methods** means how you will organise the business, approach the market and cope with changes to plan. This section should show the organisation structure, the administration and recording systems which you propose to use. It should set out the business strategy in order to identify how customers will be gained and retained, how the goods or services will be provided, how payment will be received and credit controlled to avoid bad debts. It should show any contingent liabilities you may incur by claims under warranties, guarantees or legal action and how these would be dealt with. It should also include details of any restrictions placed on the business by the parent company, such as territorial limits or the length of time granted under a fixed-term agreement. This section can also be used to summarise the benefits of the contract with the parent company.

SWOT analysis

As a summary check on your ingredients for success, consider all the information that you have gained from your research and planning. List under four separate headings all the Strengths and Weaknesses in the proposed business and the Opportunities and Threats it may face. A useful way to do this is to divide a sheet of paper into four and write down the key points under each heading. This is known as SWOT analysis and should be included in your business plan. It is invaluable as a way of looking at the relative merits and pitfalls of your proposed venture and assessing the inherent risks.

Remember that strengths should be built upon and developed; weaknesses should be recognised and minimised or circumvented; opportunities may merely represent 'jam tomorrow' unless planned for; threats (eg from competitor action, social or legal changes, or technological advances) may become very real unless anticipated and dealt with as part of your on-going business plan.

Sources of further information and advice

Companies Registration Office

England and Wales
Companies House,
Crown Way, Maindy,
Cardiff CF4 3UZ
Tel: 0222 388588

Scotland
100–102 George Street,
Edinburgh EH2 3DJ
Tel: 031-225 5774

For Department of Trade and Industry (DTI)
See your local telephone directory as there are regional offices throughout the UK.

Useful books for start-ups
Business Plans: 25 Ways to Get Yours Taken Seriously, Brian Finch (Kogan Page, 1992)
Forming a Limited Company, Patricia Clayton (Kogan Page, 4th edition, 1994)
How to Prepare a Business Plan, Edward Blackwell (Kogan Page, 2nd edition, 1993)

A full list of books on starting or running a business is available from Kogan Page, telephone 071-278 0433.

3

Cash Management, Capital and Sources of Finance

Whatever your business, getting the finances right from the start and then continuing to control them is crucial for survival. Everyone will expect you to have a firm grasp of all the financial aspects of your business, to demonstrate commercial acumen and a level of astuteness in your dealings. Much of this skill develops with experience. As with driving a car you never stop gaining experience, in varying conditions and different environments, finding safe short-cuts and roads that are new to you.

When learning to drive, the two main criteria on which you are judged to be successful are that you can drive safely and that you can anticipate other road users' behaviour. Similarly when starting up in business, it is wise to learn from experienced instructors, develop a cautious approach and learn to read the business signs.

The two main financial needs of your business are going to be cash and capital, each planned for the short-term, the medium-term and the long-term requirements for survival, stability and growth. Experienced independent accountancy advice before you start can be invaluable and will probably save considerable cost and anguish later on.

Cash

In the short term, and as an on-going requirement, your business must generate and retain cash. It is only cash which pays the bills, enabling you to meet day-to-day commitments and stay in business. Businesses often fail because they simply run out of money. Many potentially profitable ventures collapse for the want of cash planning and control.

The term cash flow aptly describes the process: that which flows out of the business must be replaced by fresh supplies flowing in!

Cash flows out through a great many ways: to pay suppliers, utilities, overheads, wages, advertising, possibly royalties, tax and VAT (where applicable), as well as interest and capital repayments on loans, dividends to investors perhaps and, not least, your own drawings. Cash may also need to be set aside regularly for replacing worn-out equipment, machinery or vehicles which have depreciated in resale value.

Against these outflows the only cash flowing into the business, other than by way of further capital injection, is that which comes from customers.

The business itself can have various 'sponges' which soak up valuable cash and prevent it from being used for other purposes. One such sponge can be the stocking of products, another the taking of credit by customers.

Stock

The nature of the business may necessitate stock-holding and this can be planned for as a working capital cost. Any decision to buy more raw material or produce stock other than that required to satisfy realistic customer expectations should be viewed as investment expenditure. In this case the proposed benefit to be gained from such outlay can be assessed against the cost of funding it and the increased risk of not achieving at least normal margin or return on investment.

Holding too much stock ties up working capital and may have practical implications for storage and handling as well as greater risks of damage or obsolescence. The costs associated with these factors, together with possible increased insurance cover, must all be taken into account. On the other hand, holding too little stock may lead to lost orders, poor customer service or expensive panic buying.

Constant monitoring of sales trends and realistic forecasting help to identify optimum stock levels, achieving the most efficient balance for the amount of cash tied up before each sale is made.

Customer credit

In a retail operation, sales are usually for cash. In some businesses sales are not normally made for cash; customers are invoiced and inevitably allowed a measure of credit. Such customers are debtors and it is important to remember that debtors are using your money all the time that your invoice remains unpaid. The amount of credit you allow to customers as a matter of course should be predetermined and clearly set out in your terms and conditions of sale. The total cash tied up as customer credit adds to the amount of working capital needed to run your business. Credit control is therefore vital to your business survival and is, in effect, the tap which turns on, and controls, the flow of available cash to your business arising from sales.

Your policies on allowing credit and the ways in which you enforce them involve balancing what is necessary to close each sale versus the risk of incurring loss through late payment or bad debt.

For each sale it is wise to consider the ability of your business to withstand the debt not being paid, or payment being delayed. Your credit policies may need to be different for different customers in order to minimise the risk of loss. Distinctions can be drawn between regular customers, new or 'one-off' buyers and the size of order involved. Obtaining a deposit and interim payments for large orders from new or existing customers can alleviate concerns over payment on both sides.

Providing a quality service and product also helps the customer to value the business relationship and may make your debt collection less difficult. Likewise, processing and delivering orders as quickly as possible, followed by accurate invoices submitted immediately after the sale has taken place, will reduce delay and possible excuses for non-payment by the customer.

Factoring may be applicable to your business as a way of reducing the amount of cash needed to service the working capital requirement allowed to debtors. It involves, in effect, the transfer of your invoices to a specialist factoring company which charges you interest on the money. This interest is described as 'discount' and factoring money can be at least as expensive as a bank overdraft. Factoring is in practice usually 'with recourse'. This means that you have not sold your invoices outright. If the factoring company does not obtain the money from your customer, it will ask you for it.

The company under whose name you are electing to trade should be able to advise you on established policies and procedures regarding the subject of customer credit and your expected management of it. Allowing customers to take unapproved credit from your business directly affects your planned cash position, shifting their working capital requirements from their business on to you and increasing yours.

Credit policy and credit control, together with stock-holding and stock control, should therefore be viewed as integral parts of your total business funding programme.

Your creditors

Those to whom you owe money are a source of funds to the business. You have the use of your suppliers' money until you pay them. Again it is a matter of balance, since paying creditors too soon increases the amount of cash involved in working capital. However, valuable discounts for early payment may be available which offset a temporary use of extra cash. Your relationship with your supplier could be soured by persistent late payment on your part and will inevitably lead to a bad reputation. This may easily translate into financial penalties on further orders to you, by way of higher price quotations or the stipulating of even more onerous terms for supply.

Creditor control, then, is also a key to cash control and astute awareness of your suppliers' own credit policies and controls can help to reduce the cash you need to have tied up in your own working capital.

Capital

The word 'capital' may be used to describe the total amount of funds required to set up and run your business, including cash. The cash required has been termed working capital. The remaining capital needed is that to be spent on fixed assets, those items which you need to buy but not sell again as part of your normal day-to-day business.

Capital expenditure can include such major items as property purchase, refurbishment, fixtures and fittings, office and other equipment, machinery and vehicles to be used by the business. There may be an up-front fee demanded by the parent company by which you purchase the right to trade legitimately under its name or trade mark.

As the business progresses further capital expenditure will undoubtedly be required, if only to replace depreciated items, the replacement cost of which exceeds the amount of any cash you may have retained for the purpose.

The parent company under whose name you trade may in any case lay down strict requirements for maintaining image, quality or safety standards after your initial launch. These may make it encumbent upon you to undertake substantial refurbishment or replacement at certain times, and at considerable cost, throughout the life of your business. Therefore, forecasting your capital requirements for as far ahead as you can see becomes a fundamental aspect of your business plan.

At this point, it is also prudent to consider what the ultimate end of your business life should look like. Many business guides and textbooks do not comment on this inevitable fate, but it is a subject well worth considering before the outset. It would be a foolish pilot who takes off on a flight not having planned how, where and when the aircraft is to be landed.

The fact that your business is flying the parent company's colours may mean that you do not have total independence of decision when it comes to sale, transfer or closure of the business. Your agreement with the parent company may well be time-bound so that you are, effectively, 'locked in'. Likewise at the end of the period of agreement, you could be 'locked out'. In this respect a fixed-term agreement could mean that your business as a whole becomes a depreciating asset, unless you can secure the rights to a major share of the goodwill or on-going income which your business generates.

Your capital planning decisions must take account of these factors, as well as what would happen in the event of your untimely demise or incapacity to fulfil your side of the agreement.

To some extent money can be viewed as a commodity: there are money 'markets' and the cost of using money can fluctuate widely according to its source, when it is drawn upon, and by whom.

The calculations of which you need to be aware are those of pay-back period and Return on Capital Employed (ROCE). Pay-back period is the forecast length of time it will take for the business to generate sufficient income to return the amount of investment to which it relates. Calculating ROCE goes beyond just finding the pay-back point and can be a useful management tool when decisions are to be made regarding possible financial investment in a business. The calculation starts with the initial cash-flow outlay, ie the amount of investment. This is followed by estimated extra cash inflows arising for each year the investment remains in use. At some point, the amount of original investment will be covered by those inflows and thereafter the investment will yield profit. By averaging out the profit over the term, it is possible to get an average annual profit which, related to the capital investment outlay, gives a crude figure for the rate of return.

The following simplified example illustrates this type of calculation:

Amount of capital investment	£10,000
Annual cash inflows:	
1st year	£2,000
2nd year	£2,250
3rd year	£2,750
4th year	£3,500
5th year	£4,500
	£15,000
Total profit	£5,000
Average profit per annum	£1,000
Return on capital employed	10 per cent

In this example, the original capital investment will apparently be covered before the end of the fourth year and the raw figure for ROCE is 10 per cent per annum.

Investors may well have minimum targets for their returns and will not lend capital finance unless realistic and further refined projected figures satisfy their criteria.

Two other concepts – gearing and interest cover – should be understood before seeking sources of finance.

Gearing is the ratio of borrowed funds to equity, which is best regarded as share capital – the stake that the proprietors, or shareholders, have in the business which is not available to be withdrawn easily. This share capital is equity whereas a temporary loan put in by shareholders to cover a specific short-term need is not. Retained earnings – profits that have been earned and kept in the business – may be regarded as equity, but it must be clear that they are not about to be paid out as dividends.

An ideal gearing for a new company would be 1:2; in other words, equity would be twice the amount of borrowed funds. However, a gearing of 1:1 is not uncommon and higher gearing may be permitted by lenders if you are taking up a proven business concept under the auspices of a reputable trading name, known to have already been successful in circumstances similar to your own.

Of course, when a business depends too much on borrowed money, interest payments can cripple it. Ideally, net trading profits, before interest and Corporation Tax, should be twice the total of interest payments.

You will also need to decide your business trading status, ie sole trader, partnership or limited company. Sole traders and partners are personally liable for all the debts of the business. A limited liability company is a business which has a separate legal identity from its founders and shareholders. Their liability for its debts is limited to the amount (usually none) unpaid on the shares they own.

The public limited company, or plc, is simply a limited company whose shares are traded on a recognised stock exchange. To help protect the interest of investors the stock exchange authorities need to be satisfied on a considerable number of points before allowing a listing. Detailed information must also be published in the required form and standards of conduct are regulated.

Sources of finance

There are many possible sources and kinds of business funding. Your enterprise may well require a varying blend of different types when you launch and then as the size or nature of your business develops.

The amount of your own investment must be considered first. Banks and other lenders like to know that the person to whom they are lending is deeply committed to the success of the enterprise; your personal monetary investment in your own capabilities and your business plan provide tangible proof of your commitment. Your money will be on the line before everyone else's, as shareholders are the last people to be paid out when a business collapses. You must be quite certain that you have considered all the likely risks and that the proposed returns will be greater than the interest you would receive by investing your cash elsewhere.

Equity

Your financial stake in your business is termed equity and represents your ownership of the enterprise. You may choose, or need, to share ownership with other stake-holders who also contribute equity capital to the business in return for shares or a partnership arrangement. Immediate thoughts turn to relatives, friends, former work colleagues and other close contacts who may be interested in helping to support the business financially. When raising capital from these sources, you must yourself be satisfied that you will be able to get along together and that you have common short-term and long-term objectives.

You may consider sharing the business ownership with some-one who has skills and experience complementary to your own. This would enable the business to be built on the combination of your joint strengths and minimise the effects of possible areas of individual lack of expertise. You may also feel happier about following advice from someone who has a financial interest in the company's survival.

If you believe that you will be able to attract outside equity finance, the Government has introduced the Enterprise Invest-ment Scheme (EIS), which allows tax benefits to people investing in British business. Details are available from your local Tax

Office, although your accountant may be a better source of advice. Launched on 1 January 1994, the Enterprise Investment Scheme replaced the former Business Expansion Scheme (BES), operated since 1981, which was failing to achieve private investment into small unquoted companies outside the property sector.

Banks and other lending institutions invest in equity, either themselves or through their subsidiary companies. Venture capital organisations exist to invest in the equity of promising companies, often with specified interests, eg investing only in high tech companies. They may insist on having their own representatives sitting as directors on your board.

You would have to comply with some fairly strict requirements regarding the provision of regular, detailed reports. The agreement would also contain provisions as to what happens if the business does badly. You could, in the last resort, find yourself pushed out of your own company if more capital is needed and you cannot provide your share.

Equity capital, then, is permanent capital for the business. As a company expands it may be the simplest, and perhaps the only, way of providing the necessary funding. The investor's shareholding percentage and the rights attached to such shares are a matter for negotiation. The investor will have an expectation of the return needed on the investment, which in many cases will depend on the risk associated with it.

Likewise, along with any other shareholders, you will know what percentage of the equity you will be content to forgo in order to give the business sound financial backing for the future.

It is in the interests of both parties to find a mutually acceptable arrangement so that you can then concentrate your energies on running the business. The level of equity percentage preferred by an investor will be determined from an assessment of the risk of the venture and its future profitability.

Although most investors will not want a controlling stake in the business, there are some situations where a number of investors will form a syndicate and together acquire more than 50 per cent of the equity. In such circumstances each investor will have a minority stake and none will have a controlling interest. Putting together a syndicate can take a great deal of time, effort and money. You are in any event expected to pay the investors' legal fees.

In most cases, then, the investor subscribes to a minority shareholding in the company. The shares are often a separate class of ordinary shares with particular rights attaching to them, particularly with regard to returns by way of dividend. That dividend entitlement will be documented and a formula agreed for its calculation. The dividend may be fixed or participating (ie linked to profits), or a combination of both.

Fixed dividends reflect the cost of money to the investor. They are therefore of a fixed annual amount, usually of an annual percentage rate similar to the interest rate that would have been charged on a long-term loan for the same amount of money.

Participating dividends are usually a percentage of the pre-tax profits of the business, the actual amount being negotiated at the outset. In some cases, the investors will define pre-tax profit as profits before shareholding directors' remuneration.

It is common for the dividend due to be the greater of the fixed or participating dividend each year. If the company does not have sufficient distributable reserves to pay either dividend, it accrues and becomes payable in full as soon as there are sufficient reserves.

However, the return that the investor hopes to make is not only by way of dividend, but also through capital gain. Capital gain comes from the sale of the business, or its flotation on the Stock Exchange or Unlisted Securities Market.

Investors may state that they need to realise their investment within a specified timescale, or they may be prepared to hold their shares indefinitely. In either case, you need to make sure that your objectives match those of the investor and vice versa. If you wish to recover full ownership, you may find that early investors with long-term objectives will not allow themselves to be bought out. Alternatively, you may be forced into relinquishing ownership at a time which suits the investor's needs rather than yours, unless you too have agreed that capital gain within that timescale is also your objective. One of the few ways to make a lot of money legally is to build up a company and then sell it, so this may well be your overall medium- to long-term objective.

Preference share capital can be used to build up the capital base of a company. However, unlike equity capital such shareholders do not share in the company's income or capital growth. The shares are commonly redeemable at a fixed price over an agreed period and have the right to a fixed dividend. The shares may also be convertible into ordinary shares in certain circumstances, eg on flotation.

Mezzanine finance combines some of the risk and reward elements of equity funding with an unsecured loan. It is used where the funding need falls outside normal bank lending criteria and is most commonly used in management buy-outs and buy-ins. The mezzanine loan carries interest, usually at about three or four points above base rate, which can vary. It is common for the borrowers of large amounts of mezzanine finance to make 'cap or swap' arrangements to protect themselves against fluctuations in interest rates. As the investment will be 'at risk' the funding often includes warrants to subscribe for ordinary shares.

Loan capital

Investors may also provide long-term loan capital as part of a package. This can enable the company to build the business free from the pressures of short-term debt. However, it is important to match the features of the loan with the need for which it is required and the life of the project.

Investment capital loans are generally available for terms of between five and twenty years. The appropriate term, repayment schedule and interest rate should be chosen with care. Often such investors will not take personal guarantees as security, preferring to secure a loan on the assets of the business.

As discussed, banks are not necessarily your first port of call for business funding to add to your own equity. However, they are usually the obvious choice for most individuals starting up in business. The best advice is to shop around, preferably before visiting your own bank manager. Presentation of your business plan is almost as important as its content; practice can improve your style and preparedness for answering questions. Also, each branch bank manager has a different discretionary lending limit. Above that limit your application may need to be processed elsewhere.

The terms of borrowing will vary from bank to bank. The period of the loan can be negotiated to match your anticipated needs and the interest rate can be fixed, variable or sometimes at a monthly managed rate. Loans require payments of interest together with a portion of the capital on a regular basis. Sometimes on larger loans it is possible to negotiate a payment holiday from repaying the capital element, so that you pay only the interest for perhaps one or two years.

Overdrafts are a common form of bank lending intended to provide for relatively short-term finance needs. Many people start up in business with the help of an overdraft facility from their bank; that is, the actual amount on loan to them varies with their day-to-day needs, although limited to an agreed maximum ceiling. The interest rate, which may be negotiated, is usually linked to base rate and is therefore variable. The amount may be calculated on a daily balance or maximum demand basis within each period.

An arranged overdraft is relatively less expensive than other types of short money and can be quick to arrange. The arranged overdraft limit should not be exceeded without the bank manager's permission. An unarranged overdraft will quickly lead to bouncing cheques, cancelled payment mandates and punitive charges.

While a loan would not be called in unless its payment terms were breached, the bank can demand instant repayment or reduction of an overdraft at any time. This could also be a consequence if the agreed ceiling were breached.

The type of funding package you can get from the bank by way of overdraft, loan(s), or both, depends on the reasons for your application, the viability of your business plan, your personal credibility, your own level of investment and the overall gearing, including any borrowing you are relying on from elsewhere. It also depends on what security you can offer as collateral.

Security

Banks lend their depositors' money, not their own, and their first duty is to their depositors. They are therefore willing to consider helping to finance a viable business plan, but not to speculate. As a consequence, banks will usually require some form of security to safeguard the money which they allow you to put at risk. If you are keen to go ahead and have assets available, this may appear no more than a formality. However, allowing the bank to have a charge over your personal assets, or those of your company, requires careful consideration. If the business fails, it could result in you losing all the assets you possess, including your home.

Even if you have formed a limited company, the bank manager is likely to require that you give a personal guarantee, in the absence of sufficient business assets. The security you may be asked for could be in the form of a floating charge over all your assets, a charge which could ultimately force you into personal bankruptcy. As a self-employed person, a sole trader or partner, you are in any event personally liable for your debts. Further, in a partnership, each partner is jointly and severally liable for all the debts, irrespective of which partner incurred them. It is strongly recommended that you have a written partnership agreement drawn up before you start trading, even between husband and wife or other family members involved as partners with you.

A written guarantee from a third party offered as security would usually be supported by a charge over property or other assets which they have. Another form of security could be a legal charge over any life policy you have which has acquired a surrender value. This would be assigned to the bank and so, in the event of your death, the bank will automatically be repaid.

Other financial assets such as a portfolio of shares in large, well-known companies can be charged to the bank if their total value exceeds the amount borrowed by a large margin, to allow for fluctuating stock market values.

A limited company can charge its property, assets, and even money owed to it, as security for a loan. This is known as a mortgage debenture and it must be registered at Companies House. The bank takes a floating charge over the assets which means that the bank has first title to the company assets, but the company can use them without affecting the security.

In 1981 the Government set up the Loan Guarantee Scheme to help small entrepreneurs who had no security to offer, such as a house, and were therefore having difficulty in borrowing money either to set up a new business or expand an existing one. Under the scheme, the Government stepped in to guarantee the lender 70 per cent of the value of loans up to £100,000 lent for periods of two to seven years. For enterprises within the Government Inner City Task Force Areas, the guarantee covered 85 per cent of the loan. The scheme meant that the lender would be able to recover these amounts from the Employment Department if the borrower went bust.

In July 1993 a new version of the scheme was launched. The percentage of loan guaranteed rose to 85 per cent throughout and the maximum loan possible for existing businesses increased to £250,000. Although the calculation for the actual rate of interest remained the same, 2.5 per cent over bank base rate, the cost of the guarantee was brought down. The premium was reduced from the equivalent of 1.75 per cent to 1.5 per cent. Another important change was the introduction of a fixed rate loan alternative under the scheme, with typical rates being 10.75 per cent for loans up to £15,000 and 10.5 per cent for larger ones up to the £250,000 ceiling. The guarantee premium became 0.5 per cent.

However, also as part of the changes, the very small businesses and many of those operating in the retail sector were no longer eligible to apply. Except for certain inner city areas, a lower limit of £5000 was introduced. The scheme was also closed to certain types of new firm setting up at the expense of an existing one in the same district. Types of new business specifically excluded from the scheme were motor vehicle repair, taxi and cab hire, hairdressing and retailing. Banks may still require a life insurance policy to be taken out by applicants to cover the amount of the loan.

Export finance

Export finance is in a field of its own. If you intend exporting, talk to your accountant and your bank manager in order to understand the ins and outs of international financial transactions.

The Export Credits Guarantee Department (ECGD) is not a financing organisation, in that it does not lend you the money to support export business. What is does is to insure your export invoices against non-payment, thus removing one of the greatest obstacles in the way of successful exporting. It is, however, essential that you contact the ECGD as early as possible before shipping goods abroad, not afterwards.

Leasing

Leasing may be worth considering in order to obtain some of your fixed assets. Although you will never own the equipment, the main advantage is that significant capital outlay is avoided, which can be a big help to cash flow. All the payments you make under the lease are treated as expenses on which you can claim full tax relief.

There are different kinds of lease. An open-ended lease allows you to end it whenever you like after the expiry of an agreed minimum period. A closed-ended one is usually for a fixed term of one to five years, after which there may be an option to take on a further lease for a nominal rent, or you may have an option to buy the item. A balloon lease lets you make part of the capital payment at the end of the lease, effectively reducing the monthly lease payments beforehand.

Contract hire

This is a form of leasing, usually negotiated to finance a fleet of vehicles or quantities of goods used in the operation of the business, eg table linen or china for caterers. Individual items are not specified, the hire covering an agreed number of an overall specification for a given period, usually with other relevant clauses included in the contract.

Hire purchase

At the end of a prescribed hire period, you gain outright ownership of the asset. As with a straightforward purchase, you can claim a capital allowance from your tax bill from the time you start using the item. It has the advantage that the capital outlay is avoided, helping cash flow. However, tax relief on the payment is only available on that portion which represents interest. The actual amount of interest payable may be at a significantly greater rate than an equivalent bank loan.

Grants and other forms of assistance

You may be able to attract grant funding, preferential loans, allowances or prizes aimed at helping small business development. These can be available from a variety of sources, including central government initiatives, local authorities wishing to encourage local enterprise and some charities specifically targeting certain groups of people or types of local industry.

A focal point now for much of the Government's assistance is your regional Training and Enterprise Council (TEC) in England and Wales or the Local Enterprise Companies (LECs) in Scotland.

Help available from TECs and LECs includes: business information, advice and counselling; financial help to assist unemployed people in starting up new businesses; a variety of courses in business skills; help with the costs of consultancy to develop staff and meet future skills needs; and help for firms wishing to train young people or adults.

In Scotland, LECs also cover help to businesses previously offered by the Scottish Development Agency and the Highlands and Islands Development Board.

Each regional TEC has its own arrangements regarding the terms of the financial support and business coaching that it offers to suitable candidates. You are therefore advised to contact your regional TEC or LEC direct (the number will be in the telephone directory). They will be pleased to send you a free information pack describing what they have to offer.

Assistance for small firms is available from a UK network of over 400 independent, privately run Local Enterprise Agencies and, in Scotland, the Enterprise Trust. All offer business advice and counselling and, in many cases, additional services such as access to loan funds, managed workspaces, business clubs and information services. They can be contacted through Business in the Community, or the Local Enterprise Development Unit in Northern Ireland.

Further government help may be available through the Loan Guarantee Scheme, as described on page 40, and special help is available in inner cities as part of the Government's Action for Cities programme. Inner City Task Forces, which operate within 16 urban areas, help small businesses with grants and loans through their Task Force Development Funds. City Action Teams coordinate Government programmes in the inner cities and can offer extra support to individual projects which are not eligible for main programme funding.

Help to small firms in certain urban areas is available from Urban Development Corporations and from the Government's Urban Programme which is run through local authorities. The programme can provide help with renting premises and with training.

You will find your local Department of Trade and Industry (DTI) office very helpful on a whole range of business issues and early contact is recommended. The regional office of the DTI will be listed in your local telephone directory.

If your business is to be located out of town, the Rural Development Commission (RDC) may be of assistance. The RDC has been helping to develop rural businesses for a number of years and will send you a useful free information pack about their programmes on request. The RDC provides businesses in rural England with free general advice and in-depth technical and professional support including skills training, for which a charge is usually made. The Commission also provides help in converting and acquiring business premises (including financial assistance in designated development areas), limited loan facilities, and grants for exhibition participation and marketing consultancy.

In addition to the service arranged by Welsh TECs, help for business in Wales is available from the Welsh Development Agency, and in mid-Wales from the Development Board for Rural Wales. These services include industrial property to rent or buy, loan and equity finance, and special help from high tech industry inward investment businesses.

In addition to the service delivered by LECs in Scotland, the Scottish Business Shop provides a range of integrated business advisory services to small businesses throughout Scotland. This includes access to government departments, company information and a franchise desk.

In Northern Ireland the Local Enterprise Development Unit (LEDU) provides comprehensive information, advisory services and financial help to small firms employing up to 50 people.

Local authorities often provide help with business start-up. Their assistance may be in the form of grants and/or loans, business advice and premises. Again, your local telephone directory is a good starting point for contacting county, borough and district councils.

In former coal-mining areas, British Coal Enterprise Ltd may be of help with loans, advice and premises. Their interest is economic regeneration of the local area, so you do not have to be a former British Coal employee to qualify for assistance.

Similarly, British Steel Industry Ltd helps businesses to start up, expand or relocate in traditional steel areas.

Help for businesses in tourism is available from the English Tourist Board and its 12 regional Tourist Boards, the Welsh Tourist Board, and, in Scotland, the Scottish Tourist Board or Highlands and Islands Enterprise.

There are grants and cheap loans available from the Prince's Youth Business Trust for young people starting up in self-employment. To qualify you need to be between 18 and 25, or 30 in the case of disabled people. Its grants are designed to cover specific items and loans, and are available towards the cost of capital equipment or to help fund working capital. A loan is usually free of interest for the first year, with a repayment holiday for the first six months. A low rate of interest is charged in years 2 and 3. The Prince's Scottish Youth Business Trust operates in Scotland.

A competition sponsored by Shell throughout the UK is also aimed at helping young people to start up in business. It is called Livewire and provides a link to free, expert, local advice and practical help. Cash awards are offered to the 'best' business plans submitted to local judging panels.

The Business Growth Challenge is targeted at owner-managers who have been in business for up to three years. The challenge is centred on the outdoor pursuit of a business management course aimed at personal growth and development. Entrants under 31 can then enter a national competition for a substantial cash prize.

In many areas, further specialised advice and business counselling is now available for women, members of ethnic minorities, and in particular those unemployed with little prospect of obtaining employment.

Instant Muscle operates in specified areas of high unemployment, concentrating on one-to-one business training, coaching and counselling for those people considered to have particular economic or special needs. It takes such people right through from considering ideas for self-employment to up to two years after they have actually launched their own business.

Sources of further information and advice

Organisations
Action for Cities
Task Force Unit
Department of the Environment
Tel: 071-276 3890

Action for Cities (City Action Teams)
Department of the Environment
Tel: 071-276 3053

Urban Programme
Tel: 071-276 4488

The Association of British Chambers of Commerce
9 Tufton Street, London SW1PY 3QB
Tel: 071-222 1555
and at:
4 Westwood House, Westwood Business Park, Coventry
CV4 8HS
Tel: 0203 694484 (Export Department and Market Research)

Association of British Insurers (ABI)
51 Gresham Street, London EC2V 7HQ
Tel: 071-600 3333

British Coal Enterprise Ltd
Edwinstowe House, Edwinstowe, Mansfield, Nottinghamshire
NG21 9PR
Tel: 0623 826833

British Steel Industry Ltd
Canterbury House, 2-6 Sydenham Road, Croydon, Surrey
CR9 2LJ
Tel: 081-686 2311

British Venture Capital Association
3 Catherine Place, London SW1E 6DX
Tel: 071-233 5212

Business in the Community
8 Stratton Street, London W1X 5FD
Tel: 071-629 1600

Scottish Business in the Community
Romano House, 43 Station Road, Corstorphine, Edinburgh
EH12 7AF
Tel: 031-334 9876

English Tourist Board
Thames Tower, Black's Road, London W6 9EL
Tel: 081-846 9000

Northern Ireland Tourist Board
St Anne's Court, 59 North Street, Belfast BT1 1ND
Tel: 0232 231221

Scottish Tourist Board
22 Ravelston Terrace, Edinburgh EH4 3EU
Tel: 031-332 2433

Wales Tourist Board
Brunel House, 2 Fitzalan Road, Cardiff CF2 1UY
Tel: 0222 499909

Highlands and Islands Enterprise
Bridge House, 20 Bridge Street, Inverness IV1 1QR
Tel: 0463 234171

The Ethnic Minority Business Development Unit (EMBDU)
London Guildhall University, Calcutta House, Old Castle
Street, London E1 7NT
Tel: 071-320 1000 ext 1204/1206/1211

Instant Muscle
Springside House, 84 North End Road, London W14 9ES
Tel: 071-603 2604

The Institute of Chartered Accountants in England and Wales
PO Box 433, Chartered Accountants' Hall, Moorgate Place,
London EC2P 2BJ
Tel: 071-920 8100

The Institute of Chartered Accountants of Scotland
27 Queen Street, Edinburgh EH2 1LA
Tel: 031-225 5673

Livewire
Hawthorn House, Forth Banks, Newcastle upon Tyne
NE1 3SG
Tel: 091-261 5584

Livewire Cymru
Freepost, Holywell CH8 7YZ

Livewire Northern Ireland
Freepost, Belfast BT15 1ER

Livewire Scotland
Freepost, Edinburgh EH12 0PE

Local Investment Networking Company (LINC)
4 Snow Hill, London EC1A 2BS
Tel: 071-236 3000

Northern Ireland Local Enterprise Development Unit
Upper Galwally, Belfast BT8 4TB
Tel: 0232 491031

Rural Development Commission
141 Castle Street, Salisbury, Wiltshire SP1 3TP
Tel: 0722 336255

Scottish Business Shop
120 Bothwell Street, Glasgow G2 7JP
Tel: 041-248 6014

Welsh Development Agency
Pearl House, Greyfriars Road, Cardiff CF1 3XX
Tel: 0222 222666

Development Board for Rural Wales
Ladywell House, Newtown, Powys SY16 1JB
Tel: 0686 626965

Women into Business
Curzon House, Church Road, Windlesham, Surrey GU20 6BH
Tel: 0276 452010

Women's Enterprise Development Agency
Unit Buildings, 54 Bratt Street, West Bromwich, Sandwell
B70 8RD
Tel: 021-525 2558

Publications

The Business Plan Workbook, Colin Barrow, Paul Barrow and Robert Brown (Kogan Page, 2nd edition, 1992)

The Cash Collection Action Kit, Philip Gegan and Jane Harrison (Kogan Page, 1990)

Financial Management for the Small Business, Colin Barrow (Kogan Page, 1988)

How to Collect Money That is Owed to You, Mel Lewis (McGraw-Hill, 1987)

Sources of Venture and Development Capital in the United Kingdom, available from Stoy Hayward, 8 Baker Street, London W1M 1DA; Tel: 071-486 5888

Tolley's Government Assistance for Business (Saffrey Champness, 2nd edition, 1989)

4

Considering the Franchise Option

Introduction

The word 'franchise' indicates that a right has been accorded for some specified purpose. For example, it can mean the right to vote. In a business context, the word may describe the right to broadcast commercial television or radio, or carry out certain operations under licence, eg the bottling and canning of soft drinks. It is also used to describe the subject of this chapter, although in this case it is more correctly termed business format franchising.

This is the type of business arrangement in which one party (the franchisor) grants a licence to another selected individual, partnership or company (the franchisee) which gives the right to trade under the trade mark and business name of the franchisor. It includes the knowledge and use of the franchisor's trade secrets and all the elements necessary to establish a previously untrained person in their own legally separate business, running it with advice and support on a predetermined basis and for a specified period. In return, the franchisee pays initial and on-going fees and agrees to be bound by the terms of the franchise agreement, operating the business strictly in accordance with the laid-down systems and operations manual.

Through business format franchising the franchisor offers the franchisee a blueprint for a successful way of carrying on all aspects of the business. The product range or service and all operational aspects should therefore have been thoroughly market-tested in pilot operations run by the franchisor.

The franchise package should thus offer a complete business format which has been tried, tested and proved. It should include not only the right to produce or sell goods or services under an established trade mark/name, but also:

- detailed product and/or service specification;
- operating systems and manuals;
- training and help to establish the business;
- business style, logo and colours;
- accounting and financial systems;
- marketing, PR and advertising support;
- continuing advice and support.

A network of like-minded investing individuals, each running the business in their own location, is created when a number of franchisees are established. Each operates to the same corporate image with the franchisor, offering customers consistency in products and/or service.

The purpose of this chapter is to introduce you to the concept and language of franchising, and signpost you to further sources of information about it. It is not to persuade you either for or against the franchise option. Rather, it seeks to provide you with a starting point from which you can make an informed decision as to whether franchising is right for you – and whether you are right for franchising!

Types of franchise within business format franchising

There is a variety of different business types within the broad definition of business format franchising:

- *Job franchise* – normally the owner is also the operator of the franchise, usually providing a mobile service, eg Home-Tune and Dyno-Rod.
- *Sales and distribution* – this often arises when a business distributes its products through its employees, eg van drivers, and then allows them to buy out and run their vans as their own business, but linked exclusively to the goods of their

previous employer. New franchisees may be recruited directly on these terms, eg the Trust Parts franchise and doorstep milk delivery.

- *Retail franchise* – franchisees are required to open retail outlets which, if warranted, may be run under employed management. Well-known examples are Body Shop, Benetton, Wimpy and Budget Rent-a-Car.
- *Investment franchise* – this is for particularly large business operations involving substantial capital expenditure. The franchisee as investor may have little or no active involvement in the day-to-day running of the business, for which he employs a management team. A current example is the Holiday Inns franchise.

Business format franchises can therefore be distinguished from other types of marketing/business arrangement and should be assessed accordingly.

It should also be noted that, in each case, the business format franchise is a comprehensive and continuing relationship in which the initial concept is always being developed. The resources available for such development are contributed by the franchisor and all the franchisees, and are therefore much more considerable than any one individual could reasonably afford or command.

The USA was the birthplace of modern franchising, where an estimated one-third of all retail sales are now made through the various forms of franchising. Franchising in the UK has developed since the 1950s, building on the history of the tied public house and our readiness to adopt American-style fast food. Despite the recent severe recession, annual sales through franchised outlets in this country dipped only marginally to £4.5 billion in 1992 from £4.8 billion in 1991. The average sales per unit were £250,000, with the figures of individual units ranging from under £10,000 to over £1 million; this reflects the diversity of opportunities available through franchising.

What sorts of franchise are available?

There are few customer-based businesses which cannot lend themselves to franchising. With nearly 400 franchisors in the UK already, operating through more than 18,000 outlets, there are plenty from which to choose – often several competing against each other in the same market sector.

Many well-known business names (and many not well known) are operated through franchises. Broad details of each can be found in various publications and directories (see pages 62–3).

An idea of the range of business activities which have been franchised, together with some of the more widely known examples of the companies involved, can be gained from the following list. (Inclusion here is for illustrative purposes only, and is not to be taken as a recommendation; nor should you interpret the exclusion of a particular company from the list as an indication of anything adverse):

- Building maintenance

  Creteprint, Dyno-Rod, Garage Door Services Associates, Gun-Point, Mixamate Concrete

- Catering and hotels

  Burger King, Kentucky Fried Chicken, McDonald's, Perfect Pizza, Wimpy, Greenalls, Holiday Inns, Climat

- Cleaning services

  Chem-Dry, Safeclean, Service Master

- Commercial and industrial

  Kwik Strip, Pirtek, Sketchley Recognition Express, Swinton Insurance Services

- Distribution, vending and wholesaling

  Catermat, Durex Vending, Chemical Express, Trust Parts

- Domestic and personal services

  Chores, Molly Maids, Poppies

- Employment agencies and training

  Alfred Marks, Travail, Pitmans Training

- Estate agencies

  Whitegates

- Parcel, courier and taxi services

  Amtrak, Apollo Despatch, Business Post, TNT, Intacab

• Quick printing and graphic design	Alpha Graphics, Kall Kwik, PDC Copyprint, Prontaprint
• Retailing	Apollo Window Blinds, Athena, Body Shop, Circle C, Decorating Den, Ryman, Snappy Snaps
• Vehicle services and petrol forecourts	Autosheen Car Valeting, Autela Components, Budget Rent-a-Car, Home-Tune, Rover, Silver Shield, Tyrefix, Esso, Jet, Shell, Texaco

The advantages of franchising

It has been said that it is possible that as many as 50 per cent of franchisees would not have become self-employed, were it not for the franchise format. Also, that the ability of franchising to help would-be small business men and women to make the transition from employee to entrepreneur is one the of major reasons for the increasing popularity of franchising.

A properly run and proven franchise will almost certainly be a less risky, more straightforward and well-planned way of going into business than setting up independently. This is because in a good franchise:

- the business concept and the existence of a market have been proven;
- the way to approach that market and how to operate the business profitably have already been worked out and tested;
- the 'know-how' is passed on to the franchisee through initial and on-going training, advice, guidance and support. Specialised knowledge in the proposed business activity is therefore not a prerequisite for the prospective franchisee.
- the franchisor should provide on-going market intelligence, since that company is in a position to monitor and analyse trends, opportunities and threats to the business. The franchisor should therefore be better placed than the individual operator to determine the overall strategic direction of the business.

The risks of business failure are thus substantially reduced. There are also various other possible business advantages.

- Finance may be more readily available to franchisees than to those setting up on their own account, because of the proven success of franchising and the track record of the franchisor.
- The lead time in making the franchise business successful may be reduced as franchisees have the immediate use of the name and reputation of the franchisor.
- Franchisees are able to make use of the franchisor's purchasing power, and there may be other benefits relating to the size of the network operations.
- Regional and national advertising and promotion can be afforded and undertaken.
- Franchisees may receive territorial protection.
- Retail franchises may have the benefit of the franchisor's strength of covenant, to help obtain leasehold premises in prime locations.
- Franchisees are the owners of their own businesses (although restrictions are imposed by their franchise agreements).

Of course, franchisors also reap benefits from the arrangements. They can generally expand their trade name and activities more quickly through franchisees than solely through their own resources. They too will enjoy the benefits of increased purchasing power for their own activities, while passing on responsibility for cash and stock security in each franchised outlet to the local franchisee. Above all, the franchisor gains commitment to the business and its customers from the investing franchisee.

The disadvantages

No form of self-employment is without risk. For the franchisee to gain the benefits of franchising, the franchisor's business and its franchise operations must be correctly structured and ethically managed.

Franchising may overcome many of the problems normally faced by new business start-ups, but there are disadvantages to be considered:

- A franchise is subject to substantial control from the franchisor.
- An initial fee is payable to the franchisor, adding to the amount of start-up capital required before launching a new business.
- On-going management service fees or royalties are payable to the franchisor; the business must be capable of supporting these and remain suitably profitable for the franchisee.
- Restrictions may be placed on the franchisee's ability to sell the franchise on, or pass it to a relative. It is usual for the franchisor to insist on assessing the proposed buyer's suitability and apply normal selection criteria before approving a transfer of ownership. Further, the franchisor may require a substantial payment should the franchise ownership be transferred.
- The franchisee's business may be adversely affected by the actions of the other franchisees and operations will be directly affected by the actions, or insolvency, of the franchisor.

Of course, the franchisor also faces certain disadvantages, particularly in divulging business know-how and entrusting the trade mark/business name to others.

What sort of people become franchisees?

Franchisees come from diverse backgrounds. Some take up a franchise following redundancy from an employer, or completion of a fixed-term contract. Others leave employment to fulfil their ambition to run their own business. Some have already been self-employed and seek the 'business umbrella' that franchising can offer.

If you are thinking of taking up a franchise, the most difficult assessment you are required to make is an assessment of yourself. In attempting to make such an assessment, you may find it worthwhile to canvass the views of others close to you who can be objective about you. Any such assessment needs to cover four main issues: motivation, personal resources, interests and personal characteristics. Use the self-assessment form in Chapter 2 (page 15) to help you towards an objective view of your personal characteristics.

It has been suggested that franchisees should possess the following characteristics (listed in order of importance):

— willingness to work hard;
— desire to succeed;
— management ability;
— financial backing;
— strong 'people' skills;
— family support.

Being part of a franchise network can offer an added advantage to working independently, particularly on a regional level: that of being in direct contact with other like-minded individuals who are in the same business. This may be of particular significance if you have a need for companionship in your endeavours, and it can help to alleviate a feeling of being 'out on your own'.

What charges will the franchisor make?

A franchisor usually requires payment of an up-front initial fee and on-going management service fees or royalties.

Initial fee

This includes the cost of buying the right to use the trading name, the provision of operating manuals and initial training for the franchisee. It helps the franchisor to recover the cost of franchisee recruitment and development of the franchise package. Often there is an element of cost towards helping the launch of the franchisee's business which, in effect, is returned to the franchisee in the form of initial extra marketing support, opening stock or specified equipment.

It is worth noting that the initial fee comprises only one element of the total initial cost faced by the franchisee. Other costs may include shopfitting, equipment, software, communications and other services, stock, transport, accountancy and legal charges, as well as the financing of working capital to be employed in the business.

Management service fee

This is an on-going fee, usually calculated as a percentage of the franchisee's gross sales net of VAT. It is paid to the franchisor in return for continuing management services, advice, guidance, coaching and support.

A low service fee is not necessarily an advantage to the franchisee. It is crucial that the franchisor retains an on-going interest in the viability and development of the franchise. Promotion and development of the business format can only be achieved by the franchisor from continuing payment by franchisees. However, it must be noted that if the costs of the enterprise to the franchisee prove higher than forecast, paying the service fee could be an onerous burden for the franchisee's business to bear.

The size of the service fee should not be underestimated because it is based on sales, not profits. If, for example, the franchisee's costs are 70 per cent of the sales value, a service fee of 10 per cent represents one-third of the profit. Also take into consideration what mark-ups, if any, are made by the franchisor on products or equipment supplied.

Mark-ups

One apparent advantage of grouping together is that buying in greater bulk can mean bigger discounts and cheaper supplies. This should also apply to franchisees, where supplies are often an important part of the cost of the enterprise. Franchisees must be aware of how the franchisor obtains profit, and it is to be hoped that the franchisor is not taking 'two bites at the cherry' by adding excessive mark-ups in addition to charging a service fee.

Royalties

A royalty is generally considered to be a financial recognition of the true ownership of the brand name by which the product or service is sold, or in consideration of the intellectual property rights involved. Royalties are also usually calculated as a percentage of turnover, or by a fixed sum charged on each unit sold.

Advertising levy

This is not an extra source of income for the franchisor. However, the franchisor may collect an on-going advertising levy from franchisees, and control the fund to help support regional or national advertising and promotional campaigns. It is usually charged as a percentage of sales, and should be separately accounted for by the franchisor. The franchisee may also be required to allocate extra funds to promote his own franchise locally.

A further financial consideration arises if and when the franchise term is to be renewed. Does the franchisor have the right to make further charges at the time, or to increase the service fee? Close scrutiny of the franchise agreement must be made at the outset to identify clearly all the financial implications of the contract.

Franchise business funding

Raising money to finance the purchase of a franchise is treated in the same way as raising money to start any new business. Some of the clearing banks have specialist franchise units and, generally, banks appear to look more favourably on the average franchise application than on the average independent start-up. This is because a franchise is believed to offer a lower risk to a lender. However, any bank or other lender will require that a prospective franchisee contributes a proportion of the start-up capital, around 30–50 per cent. Any loan, plus interest, will need to be repaid before the end of the franchise term and a bank will require collateral as security against default. If the franchise is to be run as a limited company, a charge may be put against the business assets, otherwise a mortgage or further charge on the franchisee's house is usually required.

Funding may be available from sources other than a bank (see Chapter 3). A suitably qualified independent accountant should be approached for advice regarding funding arrangements, as well as for advice on the proposed business plan and the other financial implications of becoming self-employed.

In any event, prospective franchisees are strongly urged to consult their bank and take qualified independent financial advice before signing any contract or franchise agreement.

The legal aspects involved in franchising

The franchise agreement is the document by which the franchisor controls the franchisee network. It is a legally binding contract which sets out the rights and obligations of both parties and contains provisions for certain eventualities.

Usually the franchise agreement is not negotiable, since the franchisor cannot claim to operate a coherent network if many variations of the contract exist. However, a qualified solicitor can fully explain in layman's terms the implications of each clause in the franchise agreement, which is often of weighty proportions.

It is beyond the scope of this book to go into all the legal aspects involved in franchising. Suffice to say that clauses in the agreement, which at first sight may appear onerous, are often designed to protect the franchisee's business interests as much as the franchisor's. However, there is no such thing as a standard franchise agreement, although generally it should contain certain key clauses, together with details of any defined operating territories.

Key clauses in a franchise agreement

This franchise agreement is made between   Ltd and its associate companies whose registered offices are at   as specified in Part 1 of the Schedule hereto and their successors and assignees (hereinafter called 'the Franchisor' of the One Part
and
the person, firm or company specified in Part 2 of the said Schedule (hereinafter called 'the Franchisee') of the Other Part.

---

1 Recitals
2 Rights granted
3 Term of agreement/licence
4 Rights of renewal
5 The franchisor's initial obligations

6 The franchisor's obligations
7 The franchisee's obligations
8 Training
9 Improvements
10 Licence fee and management service fee/royalty
11 Accountancy
12 Advertising
13 Insurance
14 Sale of business
15 Non-completion
16 Death of principal
17 Termination
18 Consequences of termination
19 Failure to exercise rights not to be waivered
20 Severability
21 Acknowledgement to advice given
22 Further acknowledgements
23 Warranties without authority
24 Principal's guarantee
25 Arbitration
26 Notices
27 Terms of purchase of the said products

A prospective franchisee is strongly urged to obtain independent legal advice, preferably from a solicitor experienced in franchising law, before signing any contract or agreement provided by the franchisor.

What are the next steps?

If you are confident that you have what it takes to own and run your own business, and you want to explore the possibilities of taking up a franchise, do get further advice. Read other information which is readily obtainable on franchising. Try to find out as much as you can about the market you are considering. Work out exactly how much you can personally afford to invest or have tied up in the business.

Make your own choice of advisers; do not just go to those suggested by the franchisor. Four important people at this stage will be your bank manager, an independent accountant, a solicitor (preferably one with experience of franchising), and your partner or spouse. It also pays to talk to a friend or acquaintance who has been or is self-employed, someone capable of helping you to take stock of the whole picture. Do maintain a healthy scepticism about franchises and franchisors.

Try to gather information from all angles. Some of the main high street banks have specialised franchise units offering independent advice. Talk to anyone who may have knowledge of the franchise you have in mind, the type of business you envisage, and the location in which you are thinking of operating. Also, for any franchise idea, there are usually a number of different firms competing with one another to attract recruits. It is worth telephoning a whole range of franchisors to request written details of their franchises. They all produce some form of brochure to attract applicants and will no doubt be delighted to send it to you.

You may well be invited to visit a franchisor's head office for further discussion – this is their opportunity to sell you a franchise. It is also your chance to meet them and ask questions. (A suggested list of questions is available from the British Franchise Association's information pack; see below.)

Certainly you should request the names and addresses of all existing franchisees. You can then select which ones you wish to contact yourself. After all, they are the people who are most qualified to tell you what running the franchise is like and what results you might expect from it.

Talk to as many people as you can and seek objective, independent advice and ideas. Involve your family and friends; take account of your assessment of your suitability for franchising. Running a franchise will involve a great deal of hard work and sustained effort, but it can also yield substantial rewards, enjoyment and the sense of achievement which comes from running your own business, of working for yourself, yet not *by* yourself.

Further sources of information and advice

The British Franchise Association
Franchise Chambers, Thames View, Newtown Road,
Henley-on-Thames, Oxfordshire, RG9 1HG
Tel: 0491 578049/50
Fax: 0491 573517

The BFA is the professional association representing the franchisors who are its members. It does not represent franchisees. However, it does supply a useful information pack for prospective franchisees.

Banks: The following banks provide free information packs and advice on franchising: Lloyds, Midland, National Westminster and the Royal Bank of Scotland. Barclays and the Yorkshire Bank also offer advice through their local branch managers.

Training and Enterprise Councils: Your local TEC will advise on all aspects of self-employment. See your local telephone directory for the contact number and address.

Business Franchise Magazine: A bi-monthly franchise journal which is available from all leading newsagents. The annual *Franchise Handbook* is also available.

Franchise World: This is a bi-monthly journal available on subscription. The annual *Franchise World Directory* is also available as well as a range of books on franchising. Contact the publisher: Franchise World, James House, 37 Nottingham Road, London SW17 7EA; tel: 081-767 1371; fax: 081-767 2211.

The Franchise Magazine: A franchise magazine published five times a year and available from leading newsagents.

Daily newspapers: These often carry features on franchising in their business pages.

Exhibitions: Regular franchise exhibitions are held throughout the year. There is the National Franchise Exhibition at Olympia, London and at the NEC, Birmingham; also look out for the British Franchise Exhibition, G-Mex, Manchester and Wembley.

Business library: Your local business library should stock a selection of books covering the various aspects of franchising and self-employment in general.

Useful books for prospective franchisees

Body and Soul, Anita Roddick. (Vermilion, new edition, 1992).

Franchising: A Guide for Franchisors and Franchisees, Iain Maitland (Mercury Business Paperbacks, 1991).

Lloyds Bank Small Business Guide, Sara Williams (Penguin Books, 1992; also available through your local Lloyds Bank).

Taking up a Franchise, Colin Barrow and Godfrey Golzen (Kogan Page, 10th edition, 1993).

5

Being a Commission-only Agent for Another Company

Many companies offer agency opportunities, whereby you agree to sell their products or services on a commission-only basis.

The business may allow for relatively flexible working hours, although working unsocial hours may be necessary. Agents sometimes work part time, or start off part time and then develop their activities into full-time work. Many firms will require your full-time commitment.

You will most likely need the use of a car and telephone. You will also be expected to offer commitment, energy and enthusiasm, as well as the ability to sell.

Types of agency

Companies use agents in a number of different ways and this naturally has a bearing on the type and scope of business open to you. For example, you may be offered one, or a combination, of the following types:

Sole agency   Where you are the only agent in the area for that company. This can give you a competitive edge, probably requiring full-time commitment to developing and maintaining local business on the company's behalf.

General agency Where you are one of a number of agents working on behalf of the company, having no territorial constraints or protection.

Tied agency   Where you agree to promote and sell only that company's products or services.

Free agency   Where you are free to work on behalf of other companies as well.

As an agent for products, you would not normally be expected to hold quantities of stock unless you were also the local distributor. You may, however, be required to pay for samples or your sales kit.

In the case of services, such as various types of consultancy, you may go on to provide the service to the client, or refer the business back to the company for other specialists to carry out.

Whether dealing with products or services, you may be asked by the company to supply a fidelity bond. This is an initial cash payment lodged with the company, or preferably its solicitor, as evidence of your good faith and commitment. It also pledges your agreement to confidentiality and ethical representation of the company. The amount of the bond should reflect this purpose and may therefore be several hundred pounds or more, depending on anticipated monthly commission values and the nature of the business. The bond should be refundable to you in full upon termination of your agency agreement, assuming that you have not been in breach. It should not be a form of income for the company. If the company becomes insolvent you want to be able to exercise your right to recovery. This is much easier to effect when the company's solicitor is the bond holder.

What to look out for

New UK regulations have been formulated that affect commercial agency agreements, including agencies for manufactured goods. The changes arise as part of the European Community's drive towards the introduction of legislation to a common standard throughout Member States.

As a result, all such agreements in force at 1 January 1994 and those subsequently contracted are subject to the regulations and any inconsistent term is considered void. The changes affect four main areas:

1. *Parties' rights and duties.* The regulations impose statutory obligations concerning matters which are usually implied by common law or are normally set out expressly. In particular, terms covering payment of commission are improved for the agent. Payment to the agent must be made irrespective of the time it takes for a customer to pay the principal. This outlaws the 'pay when paid' practice which transferred cash-flow concerns directly from the principal to the agent who made the sale.

   The principal must also provide the agent with statements showing how commissions have been calculated. It will *not* be possible to contract out of either of these obligations.

2. *Termination.* The regulations provide for agreements of indefinite length to be subject to minimum periods of notice. During the first year the period of notice is at least one month. During the second year, at least two months' notice is required; during the third year and thereafter, at least three months' notice is required. These provisions may *not* be excluded by agreement between the parties.

3. *Compensation.* Compensation is payable to the agent on termination by the principal, even where notice is given, as long as the agent is not in breach of any term of the agreement.

   Compensation is also payable where the agent terminates and the principal is in breach, or the agent is incapable of continuing duties under the agreement, or if the contract is frustrated. Again, these provisions may *not* be excluded form the contract.

4. *Restraint.* The regulations restrict the enforceability of restraint covenants. Almost certainly, any restraint in a commercial agency agreement for more than two years following termination will simply be void.

In any event it is wise to obtain your agency agreement in writing from the company. This should describe the type of agency and clearly set out both your rights and obligations to the company, as well as its rights and obligations to you.

Apart from details concerning the various aspects already mentioned, you will want to know what level of initial and on-going training and support you can expect to receive. Any training provided by the company may be restricted to providing product knowledge only; you may benefit from undertaking a formal course in selling as well.

Your agency agreement should clearly state who is responsible for meeting the expenses you incur as a result of being an agent for that particular company. For example, are you obliged to attend meetings called by the principal? If so, are your travel/other expenses reimbursed?

You will want to know how much paperwork you will be obliged to undertake. This should be minimal, leaving you time to pursue customers, not working as an unpaid administrator for the company. This applies particularly if you have to check out each customer's status or other details before you can take an order.

You will need to know on what grounds the company may refuse to meet the order, or refuse to make the commission payment otherwise due to you. Likewise, your commission should not be penalised by the company's failure to deliver. If it is not a cash-based business, you should also have it confirmed in writing by the company that you will not be responsible for underwriting bad debts.

The level of marketing support you can expect to receive and the company's reputation may crucially determine the level of success you can achieve, despite your own best efforts.

Payment will be by results, so you should expect to have sales targets set for you to meet and maintain.

Sources of further information and advice

British Agents Register
BAR (Agents Register) Ltd, 24 Mount Parade, Harrogate, North Yorkshire HG1 1BP
Tel: 0423 560608/9

The Institute of Sales and Marketing Management
31 Upper George Street, Luton, Bedfordshire LU1 2RD
Tel: 0582 411130 (6 lines)

6

Running a Distributorship or Dealership

Being a distributor, wholesaler, authorised dealer, stockist or merchant is not the same as being an agent, and each of these terms describes a different type of business relationship with a supplying company. As a distributor you are a customer of the supplying company, usually buying direct from it. A distributor is a type of middleman to whom a manufacturer has granted an exclusive or preferential right to buy and re-sell a specific range of products and/or services in particular markets or geographical areas. A consignment distributor is one who pays for goods only when the goods are sold on.

A wholesaler also buys, stocks and re-sells goods but without having a special relationship with particular suppliers. The wholesaler usually provides the facilities of a forward warehouse, information and advice to retailers, breaks bulk quantities into smaller units for retailing and offers a delivery service to retail outlets.

A stockist is a trader who receives trade discount and buying terms, and probably credit terms also, from a manufacturer in return for an undertaking to hold specific stock levels of a range of products. A stocking agent is another type of middleman who provides warehousing facilities and handles stocks, often in return for payment of a fixed sum retainer. The stocking agent does not purchase the goods but sells as an agent on commission.

There is a further type of arrangement, that of del credere agent. The del credere agent is one who, like a stocking agent, does not purchase the goods but, unusually, accepts responsibility for ultimate payment and pays the supplying company if the customer fails to do so. A del credere agent normally receives a higher commission than that paid to a commission agent, to compensate for the financial risk taken.

Finally, a merchant is a type of wholesaler, and sometimes retailer, who is not committed to handling goods from a particular supplier nor committed to selling to particular outlets.

In each of these types of arrangement no control is exercised by the supplying company over the selling effort, other than perhaps that of threatening to cease supply unless specific terms are agreed by written contract. The new EC Agency Directive which came into force on 1 January 1994 as Statutory Instrument 1993 No 3053, The Commercial Agents (Council Directive) Regulations 1993, applies specifically to agents. No such directive applies to distributors per se, but of course contract law can be applied in the case of any specific agreements made between parties. If you are considering signing any type of agreement you are strongly advised to seek expert legal advice beforehand.

You would also be wise to define clearly the responsibilities you plan to take on, and the terms used in any agreement between yourself and the supplying company. The following is a list of questions, specific answers to which you need to obtain before starting to trade. It is not an exhaustive list.

Dealing with stock

- Who owns the stock? As a distributor, wholesaler or stockist you will be expected to purchase initial and on-going stock.
- What is the minimum order quantity?
- What credit facility, if any, do you receive from the supplying company?
- Where will you store stock? Perhaps your garage or a spare room can be used if it provides a convenient and suitable environment in which to keep the goods. Or does the supplying company stipulate another specific type of premises?

- What security arrangements are necessary? High-value items and those of particular interest to thieves, such as cigarettes for vending machines and electrical goods, will definitely need special security. Most other items will also need some attention to security, particularly as they represent your cash investment in the business. You will want to know the exact details of the insurance policies covering the goods for which you are responsible.

- Who is responsible for insuring the goods? Adequate insurance is an essential factor in the proper running of your business.

- Will the company deliver stock to you, or will you need to fetch it? If it is delivered to you, the company should take responsibility for insuring goods in transit.

Selling and marketing

- Are you expected to deliver goods to customers? If so, what are the transport arrangements and what size of territory are you to service?

- If customers are to come to you, what premises or showroom facilities will you need, and in what sort of location?

- What marketing support will you receive, and what marketing are you obliged to undertake at your own cost?

- How are customer needs currently being satisfied?

- Who will be your main competitors and what do you know about them? Competitor analysis should be a main feature of your business plan.

- Can you appoint your own self-employed agents?

- Will you need to employ further warehousing or sales staff?

- What constraints, if any, are placed on you by the supplying company? For example, maximum or minimum selling prices, specified delivery service times, or other service parameters demanded by the supplying company.

- What is the minimum worth-while sales order size?

- What is the average sales order size currently being achieved by other dealers in the network?

As a distributor, wholesaler or stockist you will actually own the goods and therefore accept responsibility for their presentation to the customer. You will be responsible for your own contracts of sale and credit control, including any bad debts.

As an independent business, you may choose to handle products from other suppliers, including those which compete against each other. If you demand exclusivity in your distribution agreements you will need to check that such an arrangement does not infringe EC law relating to restrictive trade practices. Legal advice should be obtained regarding any demand for exclusivity by either party.

There are various reasons why a supplying company chooses to use the services of independent distributors. The goods can be made available to a much wider geographic market from stocks held much closer to the customer. Financially, there is less risk in dealing with a known number of selected customers and they, the distributors, carry all the cost of managing their own further selling operations, selling procedures, prices and the type of outlet to which the goods can be sold on are often specified in a distribution agreement.

The role of distributor or dealer is thus more complex than that of an agent and will usually incur higher costs. Your margin should therefore be higher to accommodate the extra service you are providing for the company.

Mail order catalogue agents for consumer goods

Unless the contrary is established, mail order catalogue agents for consumer goods are deemed to be outside the recent commercial agency regulations.

Notes on running a business from home

Working from home may have the advantage of convenience and low cost, but it could become highly disruptive to family life and may not create the right impression if customers have to visit.

Town planning regulations apply if you make 'a material change in the use of the land'. However, unless your business is very noisy, involves a big increase in visitors to the property, or causes annoyance to your neighbours, you may find that planning permission is unnecessary. You do need to check (probably through your solicitor) about the existence of any particular restrictive covenants on the land, and (through your insurance company or broker) about any restrictions on the insurances you have, as well as about those you will need for the business.

If you do not own your home outright, or if you rent the property, you may need the mortgagor or landlord's permission to alter the residential nature of the property to incorporate your business activity.

However, it is usually only when some part of the property is to be used *exclusively* for your business, or when it is patently obvious to the casual observer that you are running a business from your home, that objections may be raised or planning permission required.

Also, be aware that, on disposal, your home is not subject to Capital Gains Tax, whereas the sale of business premises may be. It is well worth discussing your plans with your accountant to gain advice on your optimum tax position and any other financial implications of working from your home.

Sources of further information and advice

As for Chapter 5, plus:

Running Your Own Mail Order Business, Malcolm Breckman (Kogan Page, 1992).

Lloyds Bank Small Business Guide, Sara Williams (Penguin Books, 1992; also available through your local Lloyds Bank).

Earning Money at Home, Edith Rudinger (editor) (Consumers' Association, 1989).

Home Run (published ten times a year)
Active Information, 79 Black Lion Lane, London W6 9BG
Tel: 081-741 2440.

Royal Town Planning Institute
26 Portland Place, London WIN 4BE
Tel: 071-636 9107.

Your local council planning department–free advisory leaflets are available regarding planning permission. Ask especially for the Department of Environment booklets: *Planning–A Guide for Householders* and *A Step by Step Guide to Planning Permission for Small Businesses.*

7

Being a Part of a Multi-level Marketing or Direct Selling Scheme

Multi-level marketing, also known as MLM or network marketing, has been viewed with suspicion and some misunderstanding for a long time. Yet properly run MLM schemes are not only legal and firmly established in most countries, but are becoming an increasingly popular method of doing business. However, they are not for the unwary. As with buying into any proposed business venture, you are well advised to research the company, its products and existing operators thoroughly.

The MLM concept is taught at the Harvard Business School; it is estimated that as high a proportion as 20 per cent of US millionaires, who made their fortune in the last ten years, did so through multi-level marketing.

Companies such as Amway and NSA have become recognised as leaders in their field. There are also a number of well-known party plan operations such as Avon, Ann Summers, Pippa Dee, Tupperware and Oriflame, and other direct selling companies such as Kleeneze and Betterware.

The MLM concept

Basically, a manufacturer encourages individual self-employed distributors to build a sales organisation of people like themselves, who in turn build their own organisations or 'down-line' *ad infinitum*. A small registration fee is usually payable charged to the new distributor, with further annual membership charges being required.

Distributors are paid in proportion to their own sales efforts and through their recruitment of others, with financial rewards being based on the total sales of all distributors within the organisation they have developed.

MLM is therefore big business, probably offering more people the opportunity of wealth than any other form of business, although it is not a 'get rich quick' scheme. For companies producing all types of consumable product, the prospects of having a highly motivated sales force paid by results can be attractive and likewise MLM can appeal strongly to those directly involved. It makes available potential high income for full- or part-time work with minimal financial or other risks.

Large commissions are available because the manufacturer's profits are not being used to fund a large administration/sales function and also because of residual income based on previous efforts. The idea of residual income can be likened to the continuing payments which insurance sales people, some writers and musicians etc receive, as long as the policies continue, the books or music still sell, and so on.

The most stable and successful MLM schemes are firmly based on repeat purchasing of quality products, with satisfied customers. The business thrives on everyone in the organisation buying the products regularly because they want them, or because they can sell them to end users, plus recruiting more 'down-liners' who also buy the products and recruit their own 'down-liners' etc. At the top of your own network, you gain commissions from all the product sales achieved through your organisation. Income should derive from actual product sales, not the sale of distributorships.

Pyramid selling

This is where participants have perhaps to pay relatively large sums to enter the scheme and are encouraged to purchase large consignments of goods – the larger the quantity, the larger the discount available – *before* ensuring that they have customers and further distributors to supply them to. As a result, many people are left with unsold and often unwanted goods, and are considerably out of pocket.

Pyramid selling and MLM/network marketing schemes must comply with Part XI of the Fair Trading Act 1973, the Pyramid Selling Schemes Regulations 1989 and the Pyramid Selling Schemes (Amendment) Regulations 1990.

The advantages of MLM

For the manufacturer it can be a highly cost-effective means of distribution, using the energies of individuals motivated by their own desire to earn money. For the individual, there is the potential to gain income from two sources; that is, by making commission on products sold personally and by taking a share of the profits of those 'down-line' of them.

For the sensible person the financial risk is minimal. The only outlay required is the joining fee (currently restricted by law to a maximum of £75), together with any costs which the individual chooses to invest in sales and business aids. A small annual fee may be charged for continuation of registration as a distributor.

Stock must be paid for, of course, but large quantities should not be necessary and the law requires that refunds for any unsold goods are received by anyone leaving the scheme. Many distributors cover their risk by only ordering sufficient stock to satisfy confirmed orders from customers at any one time.

If you join a proven scheme you know that the products and the methods of marketing and selling are already tried and tested. You will receive free training, advice and assistance from those 'up-line' of you, as they too will benefit from your success.

You cannot be told when, how or where to work and your working hours are flexible. There is even no need to give up other employment unless you wish to do so, although obviously the more time you can spend developing your sales, the more money you are likely to make.

By creating a large network of successful 'down-liners' of your own, you can potentially make substantial amounts of money.

The disadvantages

If you are careful not to rely on this form of income until you are confident of a steady return, and you gear your outlay in stock and sales aids to realistic proportions, there are no real financial risks.

However, people have been known to be drawn into 'hype' and over-invest in their own capabilities or unrealistic sales targets. A number of schemes encourage distributors to sell more by offering appealing discounts on larger quantities of stock. A distributor who achieves high sales one month may be reluctant to drop back to the lower commission rate in subsequent months, resulting in over-ambitious stocking levels. Recognising this, some schemes now require the distributor to meet a single fixed target only once to trigger the payment of high commissions on all subsequent orders.

The company must, of course, comply with the law and should be concerned that it maintains a reputable image. As a distributor, you are reliant upon the company's reputation for the quality of its goods and services and the image engendered by all the distributors in its network. Some companies limit the number of layers of 'down-liners' from any one distributor to five or six.

Some schemes set up in markets which can easily become saturated by their own or competitors' products. The nature of the product must also be carefully considered. 'Luxury' items may not sell well in times of recession or in particular locations. Sales figures quoted to you may have been gained in the past under more favourable conditions than those which you actually encounter. The company's marketing assumptions must be clearly thought through, and not be the result of short-term opportunism.

If you are interested in joining a MLM/network marketing scheme, direct selling or party plan scheme, you are strongly advised to obtain the relevant information packs available free from the Direct Selling Association, the DTI and the Direct Mail Services Standards Board.

Sources of further information and advice

Department of Trade and Industry
Consumer Affairs, Division 3b, 10–18 Victoria Street, London
SW1H 0NN
Tel: 071-215 3342

Direct Mail Services Standards Board
29 Eccleston Street, London SW1W 9PY
Tel: 071-824 8651

The Direct Selling Association
29 Floral Street, London WC2B 9DP
Tel: 071-497 1234

Multi Level Marketing
Peter Clothier (Kogan Page, 2nd edition, 1992).

8

Providing Financial Services on a Commission-only Basis

For the new entrant to the financial services industry providing financial services on a commission-only, self-employed basis usually means joining an established organisation to receive training, support and the licence to work under its name in return for payment by results. Examples of such companies are Allied Dunbar and Save and Prosper.

Background to the industry

The provision of financial services has grown dramatically beyond the 'foot-in-the-door/insurance salesman' image of former years. The public, employers and other business people have come to expect – and need – much more sophisticated financial advice than a generation ago. Although awareness of investment options may have increased, many people remain justifiably wary of dabbling in investment without expert knowledge.

The term 'financial services' describes the provision of advice and products relating to personal financial planning and investment and some aspects of corporate business. As such it includes life assurances and insurances, pensions, savings plans, personal equity plans, unit trusts and various other forms of investment.

Owing to the proliferation of products and the diversity of players in the market, some of whom have been noticeably less than scrupulous in their ethics, the whole industry is now more tightly regulated and controlled.

The 1986 Financial Services Act set stringent new rules for all companies and individuals dealing with financial services, although there is a balance between a wholly statutory system and one of self-regulation. Most supervisory powers have been delegated by the DTI to the Securities and Investment Board (SIB). SIB in turn relies on various self-regulatory organisations (SROs) and recognised professional bodies (RPBs) to control particular sectors of the financial services industry by enforcing rules which are binding on their members. Failure to observe these rules will call into question the fitness and properness of the practitioners concerned to carry on investment business. The Act also introduced new criminal offences carrying severe penalties, and firms must satisfy their SRO that they are honest, competent and solvent.

Of most concern to new recruits to the industry are LAUTRO, the Life Assurance and Unit Trust Regulatory Organisation, and FIMBRA, the Financial Intermediaries, Managers and Brokers Regulatory Association. Both organisations provide information packs about themselves.

FIMBRA is the umbrella group for independent financial advisers but its rules are not very different from those of LAUTRO, which oversees life assurance and unit trust sales, though FIMBRA members can sell these too. However, the leading LAUTRO players are more geared to recruiting and training people from scratch – and that creates an opportunity for those seeking a career change.

What sort of people are recruited?

Despite the complexities of personal finance, you do not have to be a wizard with numbers, or have any previous experience in financial services. The sums are all worked out for you in a sales kit, which may include a pre-programmed lap-top computer.

You will need the ability to get appointments to see prospective clients, to change their preconceptions and overcome their sales resistance. As a new recruit you may also have to work hard at overcoming your own inhibitions about selling, and have absolute faith that what you are doing is worthwhile.

Each sale should come from your ability to relate to the client, analyse personal financial circumstances and discuss future needs. The selling should result from having examined, with the client, whether proper provision has been made for those needs. Numeracy and analytical skills are useful, therefore, but general economic and business awareness are as important, helping you to relate to the client's circumstances.

As a self-employed associate, you will need to be able to absorb sufficient knowledge about the various products you are licensed to sell. Encouraged to start with 'cold' leads, ie not family or friends, you must be able to build up your own network of sales contacts and learn presentational skills. You must be relatively self-reliant and prepared to work hard. You would be expected to have already been earning over £15,000 pa in your previous employment.

The nature of the business – the need to discuss with clients their own personal finances – means that it is far from being a 9–5, weekday-only job. It can often demand an extraordinary level of dedication so, if you have a family or a partner to consider, you will need their active support in your endeavours. Typically, firms, prefer their self-employed associates to be married (or separated) rather than single. There is also a preference for home-owners. Both these factors combine, in the eyes of the recruiter, to indicate an existing degree of personal stability and motivation.

Likewise, you will be expected to divulge to the recruiter a great deal of information concerning your own financial situation, your background, and anything which may affect your professional standing or credibility and bar you from being a licensed operator within the financial services industry.

Generally, the larger well-known firms prefer to recruit people who are between 25 and 50 years of age. This is because they require mature individuals who will benefit from the training and, over time, return to them the benefits of their investment in it.

After completing the firm's detailed application form, you may be invited for a series of interviews, perhaps a further four or five, before being selected. The larger firms apply rigorous standards of selection, since recruits will operate under their name and contribute to their reputation. With really not much to choose from between products, the difference to the customer is in professionalism and service.

As all investment businesses must be authorised through membership of one of the SROs, your details will be supplied to the relevant SRO for inclusion. As such, you will be required to pass various staged tests during your initial training period, principally the Financial Advisers' Core Test (FACT) set by the Chartered Insurance Institute. Failure of the examination will bar you from working in the industry.

The full training programme is likely to last up to four years and include revision exams, so you will need to be prepared to follow it through.

These firms pride themselves on the levels of training, support, facilities and motivation which they provide to their people. The new self-employed associate should be prepared to follow the company's personal development programme and realise that measured target levels of sales performance need to be achieved.

By nature you will probably be competitive. This aspect of your character will certainly be appealed to by the firm in order to optimise your performance. Success can reap large rewards and will be readily acknowledged through increased income and status within the organisation.

What are the benefits of working with an established firm?

In terms of starting a new, self-employed career, you benefit from a parent company's provision of initial and on-going training, its back-up facilities and support. In the light of the recent legislation you also benefit from its backing in obtaining the necessary industry approval and legality.

Further benefits may come from working alongside others based at the same branch or office. Self-employment can at times be a lonely existence. Spending at least part of your time in the company of other like-minded associates may help to provide stimulation and companionship. Achievement will be recognised within the firm's motivational structure, and rewarded through higher commission rates and the opportunity to widen your scope of products and clients.

Thus the real benefits arise from on-going accumulation of product knowledge, practice, expertise and sales contacts. It is therefore necessary for both you and the firm to allow time for your efforts to be rewarded, as you gradually build up your knowledge and contacts. This is normally recognised by the firm, which will usually provide you with the benefit of flexible monthly financing and cash arrangements during your early months.

Working with a large established firm will mean that you do not require other premises or have to provide your own office facilities. You will have access to advanced systems, administration and marketing support, as well as practical working advice. Many of the risks of self-employment are thus minimised as you launch and run your own financial practice.

How are commissions calculated and paid?

Most firms follow the same uniform scale of commission and method of calculation. The commission value of each sale is worked out using a points system which takes into account the type and value of product, together with the amount, number and frequency of premiums payable. Commission is then paid at a set rate per 100 points, the rate depending on whether it is regular premium or single lump-sum business.

It is perhaps more accurate to say that you will be selling contracts rather than products. Apart from those customers paying a single lump sum, buyers undertake a contract to maintain regular payments in return for on-going benefits.

As customers do not always keep up their premium payments, a system of initial commission and accruals is operated; that is, for regular premium business the salesperson initially receives only part-payment of the total commission due. The balance is then received in stages over several years, on the anniversary of each live product sold.

This means that after the first year the salesperson's income reflects not only initial commissions from products sold that month, but also further payments for sales of 12 months ago where premiums have been kept up by the customer. However, a system of clawbacks operates too. In the case of regular premium policies lapsing within their first two years, scaled deductions are enforced and the stage payments will not be received.

Any financial assistance rendered by the company to you in your early months will be recovered by the company out of your increased monthly income in subsequent months.

If you achieve consistently higher levels of sales, the points-based commission rate increases and bonuses are paid. Income is therefore directly dependent upon results, with no upper ceiling other than that controlled for the individual by the time taken to acquire and keep satisfied customers.

What other payments or rewards can you expect?

In addition to a rising scale of commission and bonuses for sustained high performance, the larger companies provide further motivational incentives.

Annual conventions are usually held in exotic locations around the world, which the leading sales people and their spouses are invited to attend. Such holidays and other valuable prizes are not uncommon as rewards for specific success.

One-off cash payments may be made if you introduce other applicants to the organisation who are subsequently selected.

Promotion to management is achievable if that is where your ambitions lie. Managers recieve commission income based on the performance of their own self-employed team, as well as their own selling commissions. Thus your own effectiveness can be multiplied and time constraints removed to increase your income considerably.

When you choose to retire from the industry, your own portfolio of clients and the level of practice you have built up have continuing value to the company. You should therefore expect to receive payment for the practice buy-out by the company; it is important to establish at the outset how this is to be calculated.

What are the disadvantages or limitations of working in financial services?

Working under another company's name means that you rely on it to maintain a good reputation in the market-place.

Competition in the industry is strong, with a great many firms always seeking new customers. This inevitably means that potential customers are already exposed to high levels of advertising and contact from prospecting salespeople. Resistance to the cold call can therefore be high and success mainly comes through personal introductions and recommendations supported by the company's image in the eyes of the customer.

For many, working in financial services means a complete career change. It is thus essential to ensure that the move is made for the right reasons and followed up with commitment, energy and enthusiasm. The first two years can be hard and must be survived, although this can apply to any self-employment.

The industry has faced much recent legislation, with possibly more to follow. The withdrawal of licence for any reason precludes any further business.

As with any self-employed consultancy position, you will also be required to hold and maintain professional liability indemnity insurance.

What are the first steps?

Ensure that you take an objective view of your own suitability for the role. Seek, and listen to, advice from others who can offer objective comment. Talk to existing associates of the company you have in mind; meet and talk with associates from other similar companies. Make sure that you have personal support from those close to you.

The rigorous selection procedures of the larger companies should help you to decide whether you will fit in. They should also give you a clear indication of normal earnings for each stage of development, together with realistic figures of potential income.

Sources of further information and advice

Department of Trade and Industry, Insurance Division,
10–18 Victoria Street, London SW1H 0NN
Tel: 071-215 4751

FIMBRA
Hertsmere House, Hertsmere Road, London E14 4AB
Tel: 071-538 8860

LAUTRO Ltd
Centre Point, 103 New Oxford Street, London WC1A 1QH
Tel: 071-379 0444

Registry of Friendly Societies
15 Great Marlborough Street, London W1V 2AX
Tel: 071-437 9992

The Securities and Investment Board
Gavrelle House, 2–14 Bunhill Row, London EC1Y 8RA
Tel: 071-638 1240

9

Buying into an Existing Business

Overview

You may consider that buying a business which is already up and running, or a share in one, will put you on a faster route to success. Certainly, you could be trading from day one, presumably with the benefits of known products or services, an established customer base and the facilities with which to service them.

As with buying any other second-hand item, the business will already have a history over which you have had no control. To gain a viable return on your own investment, the business must be capable of improvement and have no serious defects in its make-up. Like buying a used car, unless you are a skilled mechanic or coach-builder, you will need the engine, bodywork and overall structure to be sound if you are to avoid expensive and frustrating delays to your plans.

The secret of success in buying an existing business, then, is knowing what problems to look for, and not accepting everything at face value.

To assess the financial health and 'tuning' of the business, your accountant will be your greatest ally. He or she should have access to as much detailed, documented information as possible, preferably stretching back over at least three years.

If the financial analysis exposes serious flaws such that you decide not to proceed, your investment in accounting fees will have been justified. You will have saved a great deal of otherwise wasted money, time, energy and anguish. If, however, the figures prove acceptable, you have gained vital information which can be used in deciding your purchase offer price, gaining any extra funding required and aiding your subsequent management of the business.

A limited company will have documented books of account, sufficient to satisfy the requirements of Companies House, the Inland Revenue and possibly HM Customs & Excise VAT office. A business operating under sole trader or partnership status is, however, only obliged to produce records for tax purposes. The documented evidence of the financial history of the business may therefore consist only of statements of sales and expenses, without a balance sheet. The vendor of the business may indeed claim that sales are understated, 'for tax purposes', and that the business is therefore healthier than 'officially ' documented. As such statements cannot be easily verified, they must be treated with a great deal of caution. Avoidance of tax is perfectly legal; evasion of tax is not. The business should be capable of supporting itself by legal means and not through illegal or 'creative' accounting. You should be wary of any suggestion that profits are really higher than as stated in the accounts.

Questions to ask, points to ponder

A more thorough assessment of all aspects of the business may be gained by asking the questions: who, what, where, how, when and why?

Who?

- Who actually owns the business? Creditors, lenders and other investors may be queuing for payment. Who is really behind the reason for selling the business? Buying a limited company means that you gain not only its assets, but you may also take on responsibility for any debts and liabilities remaining after the sale.
- Who owns any leases, patents, licences or franchise rights essential to the business? These may not be easily transferred to you.

- Who does the business depend on? Is the business solely founded on the current owner's personal reputation, contacts or network of business arrangements with customers, suppliers etc?
- Who else is the key to success of the business, and will they still be there when the current owner departs? Conversely, is someone causing the business to falter and will they be leaving?
- Who is the person you are dealing with? What is their background and what does their personal financial position appear to be?
- Who supplies goods and services to the business? Will they continue to supply you on the same or better terms?
- Who are the customers of the business? Who else might become customers?
- Who are the competitors of the business?
- Who can help and advise you about the purchase?
- Who else is interested in buying the business?

What?

- What exactly are you proposing to buy? What do you think you are buying?
- What exactly is being offered for sale? What are the assets which will pass to your full ownership and/or control?
- What condition are the assets in? Are they likely to need repairing, renovating or replacing in the near future and, if so, at what cost or difficulty?
- What debts or liabilities will you be taking on? What future commitments have been contracted?
- What price is being asked for the business? What are the valuations relating to stock, premises, fixtures, fittings, equipment and vehicles if these are included in the sale price as owned assets?
- What market is the business in? What products or services is it known for? What are the trends in the market?
- What reputation does the business have? What do customers say about it?

- What is the financial status of the business, past and present? What evidence is there to support the figures?
- What is the state of the competition? What will be its reaction to your trying to increase your business and gain market share?
- What effects will your ownership have on the business? Initially, trade could drop if the previous owner's personality or contacts were important factors in sustaining the business. Alternatively, you may consider that trade will improve because of your own personal contacts or attributes.
- What is the present unique selling proposition of the business, ie what makes customers buy from the current owner(s), rather than elsewhere?
- What changes, if any, would you plan in this area? What would be your unique selling proposition, your competitive edge?
- What would be your mission statement for the business? What changes would be required to fulfil the objectives of your mission statement?
- What is the current product mix, ie what products or services does the business provide to customers and what are the respective profit margins or contributions to the business from each?
- What unwanted assets of the business can be sold on straightaway to recoup some of your initial outlay?
- What proportion of income is currently spent on advertising and promotion? What would be the optimum amount?
- What price is being asked for the business? What are the main factors controlling the price? What price should you bid? What price are you prepared to go to?
- What is the current break-even figure for the business, ie what income must it gain to cover its fixed and variable costs?
- What is to become of the business? Will you sell it on, pass it over to someone else, run it out and close it down?

Where?

- Where is the business currently run from? Where might it be better located?
- Where are competitors based?

- Where do customers come from, where are customers located?
- Where will future customers be located?
- Where do profits come from?
- Where can savings be made in overheads and/or direct costs of sales?
- Where does the business currently advertise?

How?

- How are profits made?
- How is the business currently organised? How might it be better organised?
- How is the business currently administered? How might it be better administered?
- How are customers currently found? How are they communicated with, ie how is the business advertised or otherwise promoted?
- How can more customers be found? How can more sales be made?
- How can profits be increased?
- How will your purchase of the business be funded?
- How much will you need to spend on independent advice, eg accountant, solicitor, stock valuer, business consultant?
- How would you introduce changes to the business?

When?

- When would be the best time to buy the business?
- When might further funds be needed to develop the business?
- When will you achieve break-even on your investment, ie what is the pay-back period before you start to increase owner's equity?
- When do you plan to sell the business on, pass it over to someone else or close it down?

Why?

- Why is the business for sale?

- Why is the owner selling it now?
- Why are you considering buying the particular business you have in mind?
- Why has the business not gone bust? Or, if you are buying the remains of a failed business, it is important to find out exactly what caused it to run out of cash.

The question 'why' can and should be asked at every stage when considering the purchase of a particular business. It underlies the application of common sense to the situation and can explain the human context in which decisions have been made. The present owner's real motives for selling may well eventually determine the price at which the business can be bought.

Common reasons for businesses being up for sale include the following:

- The present owner is retiring because of old age or ill-health. Does this mean that the business has been run down, either on purpose or by default? Has the business been in need of investment for too long? Has the reputation of the business been seriously undermined through poor quality or service to customers before the owner has admitted that he or she cannot go on? Has the owner milked the business dry?
- Is the business going downhill? Has the market changed and moved on or disappeared? Have new competitors arrived on the scene and undermined the existing unique selling proposition by heavy price cutting or a better competitive edge?
- Is the business being mismanaged? Are the present owner's costs too high? Is the gearing wrong, so that interest payments are starving the business of cash?
- Is the business being sold off as a non-core activity from a larger company? Is this because the parent company cannot make it profitable under its own management? What accountancy policies have they been using? Accountancy practices for the benefit of a group can be quite different from those which you will want to use. Why does the larger company own it? What is the background?

- The business may be in the hands of a receiver. As such it may be advertised for sale as a going concern, but this claim needs to be thoroughly investigated. You will still need to check out the actual ownership of all the assets and whether any genuine goodwill exists. The real cause of the business failure may not be as readily apparent as its symptoms.

Buying a share in a business

Buying a share in a business can be even more hazardous, although not without its rewards if all goes well. Perhaps the compatibility of your talents with those of the other owner(s) is just what is needed to achieve success and the realisation of the ambitions of both of you.

However, none of the foregoing questions should be avoided and another should be added:

- Are you being invited to share in the business because of your experience, skills and judgement, or simply as a source of funds? If the latter, it would be perhaps more honest on the part of the vendor to invite you to invest, say, through the Government's Enterprise Investment Scheme. There will then be no dispute over business control and you can gain advantageous tax relief on your capital.

Partners working together in a business, or directors sharing ownership of a company, must have common aims for the business and be able to work alongside each other. That may sound obvious but it has to be stated because it is so crucial, not only for the survival and prosperity of the business but also for the day-to-day enjoyment of being involved in it. Ideally, joint owners should share common medium-term and long-term personal objectives regarding ownership of the firm.

If entering into a partnership, you are strongly urged to consult a good solicitor, one experienced in drawing up practical partnership agreements. This applies equally to husband and wife partnerships as to any other combination. A written agreement will help to take care of the business following unforeseen events such as the death or incapacity of a partner, or the break-up of a relationship between partners.

It must also be remembered that partners are jointly and severally liable for the debts of the business. If you have any personal assets, including equity in your home, these may be at risk irrespective of which partner incurs the debt on behalf of the business.

If you are considering buying into a limited liability company and presumably becoming a director, the bank may at some stage require a charge on your property. You will certainly be expected to take all reasonable steps to ensure that you know how your fellow directors are conducting their business, and that the company is being run ethically and with regard to the safety of others.

To some extent, this chapter has focused on the situation where you know that the business is for sale, or you have been invited into it. This should in no way stop you from considering all the steps you would take if starting up from scratch; that is, drawing up a profile of the sort of business you would like to run, carrying out your own market research and seeking independent advice.

It could well pay you to look around at similar businesses, not only as part of your research but perhaps because there are, in fact, better opportunities. Another business owner may welcome your tentative approach, even though their business is not already on the market. Banks, accountants and solicitors may be aware of such opportunities, particularly in those cases where con-fidentiality is required before a change in ownership is announced. An acquaintance who is already in the industry may have knowledge of businesses which are up for sale or open to offers. You might consider advertising in the newspapers or trade magazines for the sort of business you want. Put simply, if you are looking for the best opportunity available, the more research you can do the luckier you are likely to become.

First steps towards a management buy-out

If you are a manager in a company and believe that you and your team could run your part of the business more successfully, you might consider organising a management buy-out. Management buy-out (MBO) has become the standard term used to describe the process involving the aquisition of a controlling interest in a company, or division, by members of the incumbent management team.

For the owners, an MBO can provide a way of releasing capital otherwise tied up in the business which they wish to employ elsewhere. It also provides a way of preventing the sale going to a competitor, while at the same time continuing the company's commitment to the local community. It can provide an opportunity to reward managers for past services, avoiding their possible forced departure if the business were to be sold to someone else. If the management team is strong enough to allow major shareholders to step back, an MBO provides shareholders with a financial return for their years of investment. At the same time it allows the business to keep its identity and independence under a team of people familiar with the original owner's vision.

For the managers involved, it can offer the freedom to manage the business in their own way. They can acquire a stake in the company, sharing in the rewards of their endeavours and continuing to work in a business which they know. At times of relatively high management unemployment and job insecurity this may well have an impact on the individual's assessment of the risks involved.

MBOs are complex transactions. Usually they involve not only the buyer and seller but also a third party, the financing investor. For the investor, the MBO is an opportunity to invest in a viable business with a performance track record and a dedicated management team.

Most buy-out opportunities occur when the owners of a business decide to sell, or are made an offer by someone from outside the company. The decision to sell may have been reached owing to various circumstances and there are four main reasons:

- *Sale of an independent business*
  The owners of an independent business may have reached the point where they wish to realise their investment by selling out. The reasons may be because of new interests and/or reduced commitment on their part, retirement or even a

partner's demise. Selling the business to its existing management can be an excellent solution, especially when there is a strong emotional tie to the workforce.

- *Corporate divestment*
  There are a number of good reasons why a corporate owner may decide to sell all, or part, of its business:

  - It needs to raise cash for use elsewhere.
  - The business needs further capital but the company cannot afford, or does not wish, to inject further sums. Alternatively, it may feel that it could employ such capital more profitably elsewhere.
  - The business is a non-core activity as far as the corporate owner is concerned, deflecting resources and management time from the chosen purpose.
  - The business may not be earning the return on capital demanded by the corporate owner, and it is considered that it is not worth the effort to improve results.
  - The business may be an unwanted part of an acquisition or merger, better sold off as a non-core activity and returning some of the capital used in the purchase of the whole or for the development of merged activities.

- *Threatened take-over of company*
  The parent company may be the subject, or the likely target, of a hostile take-over bid. Subject to Stock Exchange rules where appropriate, an offer from the existing management of a subsidiary can help the main board to fight off an external offer by providing shareholders with a more attractive financial alternative.

- *Receivership*
  The receivership of a parent company may force the sale of an otherwise viable subsidiary company. Receivers are duty bound to make the most from selling the assets of the collapsed parent company and the sale of any part as a going concern should help to achieve this. It also means that if you are a member of the existing management, you are in a strong position to negotiate terms.

If you are considering the possibility of being involved in a management buy-out, the first thing to do is to check your employment contract. You will need to make sure that there is nothing in it to prevent you from approaching possible investors and the current owner(s) or directors. It is then advisable to gather further information on the subject of buy-outs; a list of contacts and recommended further reading is given at the end of this chapter. You are also referred to the first part of this chapter as most of the points raised there apply equally to the MBO.

One of the pitfalls of any buy-out is the current and short-term employer–employee relationship. By necessity you are seen to be drawn in two directions at once, pulling away independently from your employer while trying to maintain loyalty to the status quo. If you initiate discussion about the possibility of an MBO, your action may come as a complete surprise, even a shock, to those concerned. You could just as easily be considered a traitor as a saviour, with the obvious reaction.

Because of the delicacy of such a situation, the experience and advice of professional advisers and investors can be helpful, both before discussions are initiated and during negotiations. The professionals, who are used to such matters, will be able to conduct negotiations as much as possible on an arm's-length basis. This should allow you and your team to carry on performing your obligations to the parent company, while continuing to sort out your plans for the new business.

This period between initial discussion and possible culmination of all the financial and legal arrangements can be lengthy, stretching anywhere from at best, four months to, at worst, a year. Throughout this time the incumbent management are trying to do two jobs at once. On the one hand, there is a great deal of preparation: carrying out a feasibility study, producing an exhaustive up-to-date business plan, determining all facets of the change-over, obtaining and confirming the backing of investors, making all the legal arrangements and gaining support from employees, suppliers and other stake-holders. On the other hand, the business must continue to be run efficiently and effectively. Failure to attend to your normal duties and responsibilities could jeopardise the venture, or make the final buy-out much less attractive to you and your investors.

Thus, even with the help of professional advisers, much stamina, perseverance and commitment are called for from you and your team as individuals. Personalities play a crucial part in a buy-out. To a large extent investors back people more than their plans, and the experienced investors are likely to be as subjective in their opinions as they are objective about facts.

Many potential buy-outs do not get past the feasibility study. Generating sufficient net profit and cash flow to cover interest and capital repayments on borrowings, meet the debts of the business as they fall due and allow sufficient drawings for your personal needs, together with those of your team, may prove at the planning stage to be impossible. Perseverance is only justified when accompanied by realistic clarity of vision, not stubbornness.

You may not have access to sufficiently detailed knowledge of the company's financial or trading situation. Indeed, such figures may be inexorably bound up with those of the parent. The application of prudence and the preparation of a great many 'what if' forecasts will be called for. You will need excellent negotiating skills in order to deal with the current owners and interested investors.

A large proportion of the finance from investors may be in the form of interest-bearing loans. In times of high interest rates, it can be even more difficult for a business to bear the cost of the interest payable on such high gearing. An introduction to the subject of funding is outlined in Chapter 3. You are also strongly advised to seek professional advice from an accountant. This will be of further assistance when considering the tax implications which can arise as a result of how the buy-out is structured.

The way in which the deal is arranged can make a major difference to the tax liabilities of all parties. There can be tax advantages to the vendor in accepting part of the purchase price on deferred terms, which may likewise assist the cash-flow position of the new business. The tax position will also depend on whether the buy-out is completed through the purchase of the company's share capital, rather than its trading assets. Your personal tax position and that of each member of your team will also be affected. You may wish to claim tax relief on interest paid on money borrowed to purchase shares, or to ensure that a realisation profit is taxed as a capital gain rather than as income.

It is usual for the buy-out members to set up a new limited company through which they will buy the business from its existing owners. Forming the new company should be effected at an early stage and reflect the agreements between the buy-out team members and the structure of the financing package with the investor. The financial structure of the buy-out will need to conform to company law. If help is being given by a company for the acquisition of its own shares, certain specified conditions must apply and legal points be observed.

It must be remembered that the ultimate objective of a buy-out will usually be its sale, either directly to a larger organisation or by way of a Stock Exchange listing or flotation on the Unlisted Securities Market (while that route still exists). The financial resources which you and your team bring to the buy-out may well be modest in relation to the overall capital required. Your chosen investor, whether a bank, venture capital fund or other institution, will probably only lend on the expectation of an eventual capital gain from a sale or listing.

Considering a management buy-in

While a buy-out is the purchase of all or part of a business by those already working there, the management buy-in (MBI) is a similar purchase by a management team currently employed elsewhere. The most common circumstance is the buy-in of a private company from the founder or family owners. Perhaps the owner-managers have lost their original drive or the existing format has passed its peak for growth. If there is no obvious team of second-generation leaders within the business, an option may be to invite a new manager or management team to take a stake in the company. In this way the independence of the firm can be preserved while the owners receive a cash reward as well as the option of continued involvement.

The overall investment process and the structure of the new company will be similar to that pertaining to an MBO. However, there are several extra factors to consider. First, the MBI team will not have an MBO team's intimate knowledge of the company. For a non-hostile buy-in, you would have to secure honest cooperation with the vendor and, ideally, the incumbent management team in order to obtain the necessary information on which to assess the business. It is arguable whether a hostile buy-in can truly succeed, and certainly the defensive withholding of accurate information or the provision of misinformation would make the venture precariously risky for the MBI team and its investors.

The risks are in any event greater for an MBI than an MBO. The MBI leader's knowledge of the business will be less than that of the incumbent management team remaining and new relationships must be formed. A strong balance sheet would be required by any investor, to help support the settling-in period. It is not unusual for the buy-in to be led by a manager or small team from outside, which includes some of the existing management team who also gain an equity interest. This combination of MBI and MBO has become known in venture capital circles as the BIMBO.

If you can see yourself in the role of an MBO or MBI leader or team member, you are referred to Chapter 2, Ingredients for Success, as well as to the first part of this chapter. A venture of this nature still requires you to understand fully the limits of your own capabilities, as well as those of your fellow team members. Nor does it preclude you from carrying out the most thorough research into all aspects of the business and its market, if you are not to take success for granted. For an MBI leader, experience in the role of managing director should have been gained already, preferably in the same industry sector. He or she should be supported by a capable finance director, have definite leadership qualities and a clear plan for the future.

Sources of further information and advice

Buying a Shop, A St J Price (Kogan Page, 4th edition, 1989)

Croner's Reference Book for the Self-employed and Small Business (Croner Publications)

How to Buy a Business, The Daily Telegraph Guide, Peter Farrell (Kogan Page, 2nd edition, 1989)

Management Buy-Outs: A Guide for the Prospective Entrepreneur, Ian Webb (Gower, 2nd edition, 1990)

Successful Acquisition of Unquoted Companies, Barrie Pearson (Gower, 3rd edition, 1989)

The Centre for Management Buy-Out Research
School of Management and Finance, Portland Building, University of Nottingham, University Park, Nottingham NG7 2RT
Tel: 0602 515493/515494/515257

Useful free literature and further information can generally be obtained from the main high street banks and their venture capital subsidiaries, as well as from other venture capital fund-holders. Two such venture capital firms producing helpful guides to MBOs and MBIs are:

Livingstone Fisher plc
Acre House, 11–15 William Road, London NW1 3ER
Tel: 071-388 4242

and

3i plc
91 Waterloo Road, London SE1 8XP
Tel: 071-928 3131
(also with regional offices)

10

Considering a Public House

Introduction

Statistics show that nearly 70 per cent of adults in the UK visit a pub on a regular basis.

There are more than 65,000 pubs in Britain. In 1990 this figure was made up of around 29,800 tenancies and over 22,000 free traders, with the remainder under management. Since that time, further restructuring of the industry has seen a marked move towards long-term leasing schemes, which has reduced the numbers of tenancies and managed houses. At the same time, the number of free houses has been increasing.

What has prompted such restructuring is the outcome of the Monopolies and Mergers Commission's (MMC) 1989 report and the resulting Government Beer Orders. These effectively limited to 2000 the number of pubs which could be owned by any one brewer. It also relaxed the 'tie' whereby pub tenants were forced to buy products only from the brewery from which their pub was rented. Independent and chain-owned pubs are now able to offer a range of beers, which in tied houses now include at least one 'guest' beer of the publican's choice.

The whole pub sector is therefore changing and redefining itself. Social changes, demanding facilities for children and smoke-free sections, are making pubs generally more appealing to the public as the leisure industry as a whole continues to grow and develop.

It may be helpful at this point to define some of the terms used in connection with running a pub.

The *licensee* is the person to whom the licensing justices or magistrates have granted permission to sell intoxicating liquor on the premises.

A *manager* is an employee of the pub-owning company, group or brewery, receiving a salary which may be augmented by a bonus or profit-sharing scheme. Accommodation on the premises may also be provided. It is not a self-employed position.

A *tenant* is self-employed, renting the pub which is owned by the brewery or other company. It is usual for a brewery company to insist that the tenant sells the products which it makes itself and those for which it has agreed national distribution from other firms providing complementary products. The MMC report has led to the relaxation of some of the previously tighter restrictions of the tie.

A *free trader* is one who owns a free house; that is, a self-employed person who owns and operates their own independent pub, free of any tie to a particular brewery company. The pub premises themselves may be owned by the free trader either as freehold or leasehold.

Since the 1989 Government Beer Orders, the larger brewery companies have mostly developed a concept of brewery leases or, in some cases, business format franchises. The brewery lease or franchise overcomes aspects of criticism contained in the MMC report by devolving operational ownership to a longer-term leaseholder or franchisee. The term is usually 20 years, although there are leases and franchises available for ten-year terms usually with a further five-year option.

Overview of the advantages and disadvantages of each type of agreement

The range of agreements described above allows for self-employment in the industry at almost every level of ownership. However, each type of arrangement can hold advantages and disadvantages for the prospective publican.

Tenancy

The tenant usually undertakes a minimum three-year legally binding contract. The pub premises are rented from the brewery company and there is normally a tie involved. However, the company is generally responsible for the upkeep, decoration and insurance of the buildings, although sometimes the tenant is responsible for the living quarters. The tie can extend to the supply and running of fruit machines and other pub amusement equipment, from which a proportion of the profit is retained. Such equipment is usually separately leased, but forms part of the tenancy package. The brewery company will probably ensure that the tenant undertakes a formal course of basic training, and will then provide on-going business advice and merchandising support for its products.

If you are thinking of taking a tenancy, you will require capital to cover the 'in-goings'; that is, the sum agreed by the valuers on behalf of the outgoing licensees to cover fixtures and fittings, furnishings and stock. In-goings will also need to cover payment of the stocktaker's fees, the valuer's fees, the purchase of any optional items from the outgoing tenant and, most important, working capital. The total sum is usually in the region of £10,000 to £12,000, but could be up to £40,000 depending on the quality of the goods and the volume of trade. You will also need to cover the cost of any accountant's or solicitor's fees that you incur in assessing the business before purchase.

Tenancy rents are usually calculated on the basis of the annual number of barrels of beer sold through the pub. This appears fair enough, but it does mean that if you go through a rent review after, say, your first three years, your rent will be increased in line with how much you have increased your trade.

Another downside is that with a tenancy you are not building an appreciating asset. Indeed, the fixtures and fittings in which you invested at the start of your tenancy will have depreciated in value, and you will not be able to capitalise on any goodwill that you may have built up. You will therefore need to have made provision for your move out of the tenancy, towards your pension and your next home. The wise tenant keeps an eye on the implications of inflation and changes in the housing market.

In the meantime, from a relatively modest capital investment, you may well enjoy a reasonable standard of living, with opportunities to develop it further through your own endeavours.

To apply for a tenancy, you can approach brewery companies direct, contact licensed property brokers (pub 'estate agents') and/or follow up advertisements in the press and trade papers. As when considering any business opportunity, you are advised to seek knowledgeable guidance and weigh up as many alternative options as possible.

Free house

As a free trader you will own and operate your own independent pub. This means that you are solely responsible for the upkeep, improvement and insurance of the premises, which are usually freehold, as well as for everything they contain. In view of the often distinctive age and construction (with subsequent altera- tions) of most free houses, you would be wise to obtain thorough surveys on any particular premises that you consider buying.

The pointers already given in Chapter 9, Buying into an Existing Business, are all relevant here. Before investing in a pub, particularly where substantial funds are required to purchase a free house, you would be wise to talk to the local police as part of your research. They may well have valuable information about local trading conditions and will certainly know of any previous problems which may have arisen with customers. In any case, it is sensible to get to know the local constabulary and establish good terms from the start.

As there is no tie imposed on a free house, you are able to choose supplies from any source. However, this also means that you have no particular company with a vested interest in your survival. You will need to be confident that you are already adequately trained and experienced enough to handle all aspects of the business. This includes having the skills to recruit, train and manage the staff you will need, as well as the business and technical abilities demanded by being your own boss.

You may be able to obtain point-of-sale merchandising material from your suppliers to support their product lines. You will also be free to take advantage of any special offers or trade promotions available from the whole range of suppliers and distributors.

As a free trader you have complete freedom to decide your own house 'style' and you retain all the profits from any amusement machines, entertainment or catering which you provide for customers. You would be building an appreciating asset, assuming that there is no major drop in property values. On selling the business you would be able to capitalise on the goodwill you have yourself generated in the business. Being self-employed, you may still want to make your own pension provisions, but the sale of the pub should at least recoup your capital investment for the purchase of your next home. However, as with any business, periods of recession or an unexpected decline in local trade caused by factors beyond your control can play havoc with the best laid plans.

The cost of your original investment in a free house can be any amount from £60,000 upwards. It is important to remember that you get what you pay for and the cheapest may not be the best. As in any other form of retailing, location can be the key and, once decided, cannot be altered. The premises themselves, however, may be capable of substantial improvement. According to trade estimates, the average cost of a freehold pub in 1989 was around £275,000. Since then, recession has caused prices to drop back but the free pub remains a much sought-after prize and the laws of supply and demand dictate their own terms.

Licensed property brokers and the trade press are the usual sources of information about premises for sale, but you may be well advised to develop your own network of contacts in order to be informed of imminent properties coming on to the market.

Lease

As previously mentioned, there has been a trend towards long-term leases as a result of the 1989 MMC report. Some of the schemes have received recent unfavourable press comments owing mainly to provisions for upwards-only rent reviews after their first three years. Some leases signed at the height of the market in 1989/90 became untenable in the recession which immediately followed.

A further cause for concern was the way in which some of these problems for lessees were dealt with by particular brewery companies, especially those which had built into their leases penalty clauses for under-achievement of sales targets.

It must be remembered, however, that the maxim 'buyer beware' still applies. A legally binding contract should be entered into with good faith but with eyes wide open to all the implications.

The modern brewery lease can be entered into by sole traders, partners or companies, with guarantors required as appropriate and nearly always in the case of companies. The term is often initially advertised as being for 20 years, but ten-year leases with optional five-year renewals have become available from some breweries.

Usually no premium is charged for the lease, which is generally assignable after two or three years with the brewery company's consent. It is important to note that under current English law, should you assign the lease, you remain responsible for payments under the terms of the lease in the event of failure by the assignee. Sub-letting is usually prohibited under the terms of the lease, as is assignment to other brewers. Rent is usually required to be paid quarterly in advance by variable direct debit.

The rent will be determined according to the anticipated level of trade, with some brewers demanding a minimum purchase obligation (MPO) from the lessee. As mentioned, instances have already arisen where licensees have failed to meet the pre-set targets and found themselves seriously penalised financially. Not all breweries impose such penalties and some tackle the need to achieve targets by the opposite method of giving incentives through discount schemes.

One of the main conditions in a lease will be that the lessee is fully responsible for repairing and insuring; that is, you will have to put and keep the property in good and substantial repair at your cost throughout the term. Voluntary authorised improvements which increase the rental value are normally disregarded from rent reviews. Improving the property may increase your trade or business efficiency, but you would need to achieve a suitable return within the life of the lease. This is because such improvements generally become the property of the brewery at the end of the lease, without any recompense to you. Likewise, the lease arrangement does not recognise any goodwill value which you might otherwise have felt you deserved. The lease is a depreciating asset and similar circumstances apply as for a tenancy, although ownership of fixtures and fittings revert to the brewery at no cost on expiration of the lease.

The buildings will normally be insured by the brewery company, but the bill will be passed to you for reimbursement. Insurance will also be required to cover up to three years' payment of rent and loss of licence.

The lease is likely to involve a tie to the brewery company's products, just like a tenancy agreement, although you will probably retain all profits from pub amusement machines, entertainment, special events and catering. The brewery usually reserves the right to waive the tie and may become legally obliged to do so in the future. In this event, there would be provision for an interim rent review, other than at the normal three- or five-year intervals, and the rent would, of course, be significantly marked up.

A lease normally requires you to pay the legal fees of both parties and you would be responsible for all outgoings, including those for your accommodation, water, heat, light and power and the business rates charged by the local authority.

In summary, then, a lease may enable you to obtain suitable premises which you may not otherwise be able to afford, or want, to buy. It is not something to be entered into lightly. Although you will no doubt receive initial and on-going training, advice and guidance from the brewery company, you would be wise to seek professional legal and financial advice beforehand.

As with the purchase of a free house, you are strongly urged to draw up a realistic business plan and heed advice from others already in the trade.

To apply for a lease, you would normally contact the brewery company direct or through their appointed agents. The Association of Valuers of Licensed Property can also advise on the availability of premises.

What sort of people become licensees?

People from all backgrounds have been successful in the pub trade and, for many, running their own pub makes a rewarding second career. Running a pub is often seen as a job for two or more people, and many brewers and pub chains prefer to receive such joint applications for tenancies and leases. Couples with young children should satisfy themselves that they can cope with family demands both during initial training and throughout the life of their business.

The legal minimum age for selling alcohol is 18, but it is unlikely that a tenancy or lease would be granted to anyone under 25 years of age.

As with other forms of self-employment, particular personal qualities, attributes and communication skills are called for, as described in Chapter 2, Ingredients for Success. Running a pub additionally requires a high tolerance of and a positive liking for the public. It calls for pleasant, polite and friendly characteristics coupled with a readiness to work long, unsocial hours and a willingness to be constantly cleaning and tidying up after customers.

The rewards can be almost limitless and are usually measured by publicans in terms of job enjoyment as well as financial return. It is most definitely a whole way of life, not merely a job.

Sources of further information and advice

Organisations
The Association of Valuers of Licensed Property
310 Ewell Road, Surbiton, Surrey KT6 7AL
Tel: 081-390 7833

The Brewers Society
42 Portman Square, London W1H 0BB
Tel: 071-486 4831 (16 lines)

The British Institute of Inn-Keeping
51–53 High Street, Camberley, Surrey GU15 3RG
Tel: 0276 684449

Federation of Licensed Victuallers Association
126 Bradford Road, Brighouse, West Yorkshire HD6 4AU
Tel: 0484 710534

Hotel and Catering Training Company
International House, High Street, London W5 5DB
Tel: 081-579 2400

The Scottish Licensed Trade Association
10 Walker Street, Edinburgh EH3 7LA
Tel: 031-225 5169

Books
An ABC of Licensing Law,
The Morning Advertiser (address below)

Inn-keeping – A Manual for Licensed Victuallers,
Brewing Publications Ltd (The Brewers Society; see above for
address)

Running Your Own Pub,
Elven Money (Kogan Page, second edition, 1992)

Thinking of Buying a Pub,
Christie & Co, 50 Victoria Street, London SW1H 0NW;
Tel: 071-799 2121

Journals and trade press
Caterer and Hotelkeeper
Quadrant House, The Quadrant, Sutton, Surrey SM2 5AS

Free House Monthly
47 Church Street, Barnsley S70 2AS

Inn-Keeping Today
Journal of British Institute of Inn-Keeping, 42 Portman Square,
London W1H 0BB

Licensee and Free Trader
The Morning Advertiser, Elvian House, Nixey Close, Slough,
Berkshire SL1 1NQ

The Publican
29 Lower Coombe Street, Croydon, Surrey CR9 1LX

Index